Character Builders

Character Builders

Books and Activities for
Character Education

Liz Knowles, Ed.D. and Martha Smith

A Member of the Greenwood Publishing Group

Westport, Connecticut • London

Library of Congress Cataloging-in-Publication Data

Knowles, Elizabeth, 1946-
  Character builders : books and activities for character education / by Liz Knowles and Martha Smith.
      p. cm.
  Includes bibliographical references and index.
  ISBN 1-59158-370-5 (pbk. : alk. paper)
  1. Moral education—United States. 2. Character—Study and teaching—United States. 3. Children's literature—Moral and ethical aspects. 4. Children—Books and reading—United States. 5. Children's literature, American—Bibliography. I. Smith, Martha. II. Title.
LC311.K59 2006
  370.11'4—dc22   2006017626

British Library Cataloguing in Publication Data is available.

Library of Congress Catalog Card Number: 2006017626
ISBN: 1-59158-370-5

First published in 2006

Libraries Unlimited, 88 Post Road West, Westport, CT 06881
A Member of the Greenwood Publishing Group, Inc.
www.lu.com

Printed in the United States of America

The paper used in this book complies with the Permanent Paper Standard issued by the National Information Standards Organization (Z39.48–1984).

10   9   8   7   6   5   4   3   2   1

Contents

Introduction

Why This Topic?

As parents and teachers, we are constantly involved in character education. We model our character traits every day whether we realize it or not. Often we do not realize that children are closely watching what we do and say, how we act and react. Even though we think we are clearly focusing on character development in our homes and schools, we only have to read the newspaper or watch the nightly news to see that more needs to be done.

Children need the assistance of adults to learn moral and proper behavior. Children are always watching and mindful of what is happening around them, and in the early stages of their development they are very impressionable.

Bohlin, Farmer, and Ryan in *Building Character in Schools* (Jossey-Bass, 2001) state that character education is not simply a movement or a fad, but that it is central to good teaching and learning. It is about helping our students make wise decisions and then to act on them. Character education is respectful of different cultures, religions, and creeds.

Brooks and Goble, in *The Case for Character Education: The Role of the School in Teaching Values and Virtue* (Quick Publishing, 1998), advise that because of the changing structure of the American family, changing approaches to child rearing, and the powerful influences of media on the character of students, there is now an even greater need for ethical behavior to be taught by schools today.

According to Dictionary.com (http://www.dictionary.com), *character* is the combination of qualities or features that distinguishes one person, group, or thing from another; it is also defined as moral or ethical strength. *Virtue* means moral excellence and righteousness; goodness and particularly efficacious, good, or beneficial quality.

In our school community, we have begun to focus on a specific character trait each month. This is not to say that we don't recognize opportunities to work on other traits at the same time, but we felt it was important that our entire community come together to focus on a trait a month. Because we greatly value reading in our school, we wanted to provide literature connections to character traits for teachers and for the parents of all our students. In searching for resources, we were unable to find one source that provided current and classic titles for all ages, from pre-K to grade 12, categorized by main character trait.

How Can You Use the Resources in This Book?

This resource can be used to support an existing character education program by identifying literature that exemplifies the twelve virtues. Each chapter can be used as a stand-alone so that you can customize the book to fit your needs. In this way, you can support your character education program with a pleasurable experience—reading—paired with discussion guided by open-ended questions. We also suggest that you share these titles within the framework of literature circles or book clubs. The rationales for these choices include positive feelings about reading, making personal connections with literature, and working cooperatively in groups.

Literature circles and book clubs are described at length in the following teacher resource books:

Daniels, Harvey. *Literature Circles: Voice and Choice in Book Clubs and Reading Groups.* Stenhouse Publishers, 2002. ISBN 1-57110-333-8

Daniels, Harvey. *Literature Circles: Voice and Choice in the Student-Centered Classroom.* Stenhouse Publishers, 1994. ISBN 1-57110-000-8

Day, Jeni Pollack (ed.) *Moving Forward with Literature Circles: How to Plan, Manage, and Evaluate Literature Circles to Deepen Understanding and Foster a Love of Reading.* Scholastic Professional Books, 2002. ISBN 0-439-17668-9

Hill, Bonnie Campbell, Katherine L. Schlick Noe, and Nancy J. Johnson. *Literature Circles Resource Guide: Teaching Suggestions, Forms, Sample Book Lists, and Database.* Christopher-Gordon Publishers, 2000. ISBN 1-929024-23-1

Knowles, Elizabeth, and Martha Smith. *Talk about Books!: A Guide for Book Clubs, Literature Circles, and Discussion Groups, Grades 4–8.* Libraries Unlimited, 2003. ISBN 1-59158-023-4

Neamen, Mimi, and Mary Strong. *More Literature Circles: Cooperative Learning for Grades 3–8.* Libraries Unlimited, 2001. ISBN 1-56308-895-9

Noe, Katherine L. Schlick, and Nancy J. Johnson. *Getting Started with Literature Circles.* Christopher-Gordon Publishers, 1999. ISBN 0-926842-97-8

Raphael, Taffy E., Marcella Kehus, and Karen Damphousse. *Book Club for Middle School.* Small Planet Communications, 2001. ISBN 0-9656211-2-X

Raphael, Taffy E., Laura S. Pardo, and Kathy Highfield. *Book Club: A Literature-Based Curriculum.* Small Planet Communications, 2002. ISBN 1-931376-07-7

After adding these titles to our professional or personal libraries and reading them from cover to cover and then working with teachers at many grade levels who wanted to try literature circles or book clubs, we put together these guidelines for using this approach:

1. The teacher introduces the book titles that are available and has up to six copies of each if the media specialist's budget allows.

2. The groups are formed by student choice (the teacher may want to "help" to ensure an appropriate mix in each group).

3. The size of the group can range from three to five students (the choice is up to the teacher).

4. The teacher determines the overall time frame for completing the book (to fit in with vacations, special events, curriculum, etc.).

5. Each group decides how much of the book to read for homework each night.

6. The teacher decides whether each group member should have an assigned responsibility for enhancing the discussion.

7. Each group member has a role or task (after looking at all the options suggested in the resource books, each teacher makes choices—sometimes not using any roles or making up his or her own).

8. Each group member keeps a journal or uses sticky notes for notations of questions, selections for discussion, comments, and illustrations (some sort of writing should be included).

9.   Open-ended discussion questions are posted around the classroom (make sure there are boy-friendly questions, too).

10.   Students may share their book with the rest of the class at the end or do a project or activity (the teacher decides whether this is necessary and what form this project will take).

11.   Students overhearing discussions and seeing projects are likely to read the book on their own to find out what the other students were talking about.

12.   New literature circles are formed when new titles are offered.

Open-ended discussion questions are very important to encourage the students to think about and share the books they read. Allow them to read and discuss, draw parallels and examples, and discover strengths and weaknesses. Do not ask literal comprehension questions, quiz vocabulary, or provide fill-in worksheets to determine whether the students are really reading their books. Create project ideas that might serve as a culminating activity. The following are some teacher resources with project ideas.

Moen, Christine Boardman. *Better than Book Reports: More than 40 Creative Responses to Literature.* Scholastic Professional Books, 1992. ISBN 0-590-49213-6

O'Brien-Palmer, Michelle. *Beyond Book Reports: 50 Totally Terrific Literature Response Activities the Develop Great Readers and Writers.* Scholastic Professional Books, 1997. ISBN 0-590-76991-X

http://www.teachnet.com has three lists, each with over 150 ideas, called "More Ideas than You'll Ever Use for Book Reports!"

The bottom line is to get students to read and make a personal connection to the book and provide a venue to discuss the virtue as an integral part of your character education plan.

How Are the Titles Organized?

The titles are divided into six categories:

Picture Books

Primary (grades 1–3)

Intermediate (grades 3–5)

Middle School (grades 5–8)

Young Adult (grades 8–12)

Nonfiction

The grade levels in the categories overlap because there are a wide range of reading levels and interests in each category and there should be no restrictions. The grade levels were determined using *Books in Print* and *School Library Journal*.

What Sources Were Consulted?

We examined a number of titles dealing strictly with character education to develop a list of twelve character traits for this book. The most complete list was compiled by Spencer Kagan, in *Smart Card: Character Education* (Kagan Publishing, 1999, p. 1). This list included ninety-eight virtues from A to Z. Kagan says, "Character education is an intentional, systematic effort to identify and foster in students positive virtues such as caring, cooperation, respect, responsibility, honesty, integrity—virtues fundamental to the development of good character. Character education transmits a shared moral and ethical heritage crucial to the preservation and vitality of a civilized democratic society." Kagan's twelve most important virtues are caring, citizenship, cooperation, courage, fairness, honesty, integrity, leadership, loyalty, perseverance, respect, and responsibility.

In *The Book of Virtues* (Simon & Shuster, 1993, p. 11), William J. Bennett states, "moral education is the training of heart and mind toward the good. Along with precept, habit, and example there is also a need for moral literacy." His list of virtues includes self-discipline, compassion, responsibility, friendship, work, courage, perseverance, honesty, loyalty, and faith.

Sharron L. McElmeel's *Character Education: A Book Guide for Teachers, Librarians, and Parents* (Libraries Unlimited, 2002, p. xii) says, "In recent years there has been a return to 'character education' discussions of values and appropriate behavior in our nation's classrooms. Children's literature provides us with convenient and effective tools for instigating discussions about specific and desirable character traits." Her list of traits and virtues consists of caring, confidence, courage, curiosity, flexibility, friendship, goal setting, humility, humor, initiative, integrity, patience, perseverance, positive attitude, problem solving, self-discipline, and team work.

John Heidel and Marion Lyman-Anderson in *Character Education* (Incentive Publications, 1999, p. 10) provide a character education curriculum for K–6 and then for grades 6–12 that spans two years and covers many virtues. "Since one of the primary concerns of this program specifically relates to the total development of students, it is important to remember what a complete student is. A complete student is one who succeeds academically, but also portrays a strong moral character, with a clear sense of right and wrong." The virtues covered over two years are respect, responsibility, compassion, faith, commitment, love, wisdom, health, humor, honesty, cooperation, humility, peace, patience, courage, creativity, environmental awareness, and freedom.

In *Educating for Character: How Our Schools Can Teach Respect and Responsibility* (Bantam Books, 1992, pp. 3–4), Dr. Thomas Lickona states, "Escalating moral problems in society ranging from greed and dishonesty to violent crime to self-destructive behaviors such as drug abuse and suicide are bringing about a new consensus. Now from all across the country, from private citizens and public organizations, from liberals and conservatives alike comes a summons to the schools: Take up the role of moral teachers of our children."

In *Character Matters: How to Help Our Children Develop Good Judgment, Integrity, and Other Essential Virtues* (Simon & Schuster, 2004, p. 5), Lickona says, "Character is having the 'right stuff.' As parents and educators we labor to teach kids that it's what's inside that counts." He lists ten essential virtues: wisdom, justice, fortitude, self-control, love, positive attitude, hard work, integrity, gratitude, and humility.

Barbara A. Lewis in *What Do You Stand For? A Kids' Guide to Building Character* (Free Spirit Publishing, 1998, p. 1), says, "Positive character traits are something you can and should develop. There is a core group of character traits that every member of the human family needs to have." Her list of traits contains caring, choice, citizenship, cleanliness, communication, conservation, courage, empathy, endurance, forgiveness, health, honesty, imagination, integrity, justice, leadership, loyalty, peacefulness, problem solving, purpose, relationships, respect, responsibility, safety, self-discipline, and wisdom.

Pam Schiller and Tamera Bryant, in *The Values Book: Teaching 16 Basic Values to Young Children* (Gryphon House, 1998, p. 6), make these statements: "American society is changing rapidly. Technology, our socioeconomic structure, our family structure and our business culture are just a few of the areas that have changed dramatically over the past twenty years. Each of these changes has created and continues to create its own ripple effect in our attitudes and behaviors." Their sixteen basic values are commitment, compassion, cooperation, courage, fairness, helpfulness, honesty, humor, integrity, loyalty, patience, pride, respect, responsibility, self-reliance, and tolerance.

Barbara Unell and Jerry Wycoff's *20 Teachable Virtues: Practical Ways to Pass on Lessons of Virtue and Character to Your Children* (Berkley Publishing, 1995, p. xvi) claims, "This book is testimony to a celebration of the fact that we are each in charge of preventing and/or cleaning up the mess of our character-starved, immorally-littered world." The twenty virtues in this work are empathy, helpfulness, fairness, tolerance, caring, courage, humor, respect, loyalty, courtesy, patience, resourcefulness, peacemaking, self-reliance, self-motivation, responsibility, honesty, trustworthiness, self-discipline, and cooperation.

Diane Findlay, in *Characters with Character: Using Children's Literature in Character Education* (Alleyside Press, 2001, p. 5), says, "Character education, at its most universal, involves consciously nurturing in students core ethical values, which can be seen as basic skills for productive, successful living in a diverse and rapidly changing world." Her list of virtues consists of respect, responsibility, caring, honesty, perseverance, courage, self-discipline, fairness, friendship, and citizenship.

Colin Greer and Herbert Kohl, in *A Call to Character: A Family Treasury of Stories, Poems, Plays, Proverbs, and Fables to Guide the Development of Values for You and Your Children* (Harper Perennial, 1995, p. 1), say that "Character develops and is tested throughout life; it is not fixed once and for all. Self-respect is tested during hard times, and there are moments when compassion conflicts with self-interest. It is not easy to be consistently honest if one feels deprived. Loyalty to family and friends can often contradict loyalty to ideas or principles." Virtues covered by these authors include courage, self-discipline, integrity, creativity, playfulness, loyalty, generosity, empathy, honesty, adaptability, idealism, compassion, responsibility, balance, fairness, and love.

Edward DeRoche and Mary Williams, in *Character Education: A Primer for Teachers* (Argus Communications, 2001, p. 5), advise, "If character is learned and it involves one's experiences and relationships, then schools have a role to play. Schools are the one place where children and youth come together to learn, examine, and apply positive character traits." They select the following six traits: respect, effort, responsibility, kindness, trustworthiness, and honesty.

In *Books That Build Character: A Guide to Teaching Your Child Moral Values through Stories* (Touchtone Books, 1994, p. 17), William Kilpatrick and Gregory and Suzanne Wolfe state, "There are thousands of finely crafted stories for children that make honesty, responsibility, and compassion come alive. But they are not always easy to find. Concepts such as virtue, good example, and character have been out of fashion in our society for some time, and their absence is reflected in the available guidebooks to children's literature."

What Character Education Web Sites Were Reviewed?

Good Character.com
http://www.goodcharacter.com

This Web site provides teaching guides for K–12, information about service learning, character in sports, great Web resources for teachers, school to work ethic in the workplace, materials for leading quality classroom discussions, and links to important character education organizations. The Web site is guided by six important character principles. It has a store and offers character education materials for sale.

National Character Education Center
http://www.ethicsusa.com

The founder and CEO of the National Character Education Center is Gene Bedley, an educator with thirty-three years of service in public schools. He is the author of a number of books on values and discipline. This organization provides information and seminars on character education and awards leaders in character education annually through its National Educator Awards Program. On the Web site you can order the *Values in Action* program and free newsletters and also visit a bookstore.

Character Counts!
http://www.charactercounts.org

This organization was founded in 1993 by the Josephson Institute of Ethics, a nonsectarian, non-profit, public-benefit organization, after a 1992 conference in Aspen, Colorado. A diverse group of ethicists, educators, and youth-service professionals attended the Aspen conference looking for a way to get together and boost their character education efforts. The Aspen Declaration, a set of eight guiding principles, became the foundation for the Character Counts program. This program is identified by its six pillars: trustworthiness, respect, responsibility, fairness, caring, and citizenship. Character Counts has almost six thousand members that include national organizations, school districts and educational organizations, individual schools, communities, cities, counties, service organizations, businesses, and children's activity centers. On the Web site you can join the organization, sign up for training and free newsletters, and shop online for their many materials.

The Character Education Partnership
http://www.character.org

Character Education Partnership (CEP), based in Washington, D.C., is a nonprofit, nonpartisan, nonsectarian, coalition of organizations and individuals working to foster excellent character education programs in our nation's schools. CEP has created Eleven Principles of Effective Character Education and Character Education Quality Standards—guidelines to assist schools in their development of quality programs. CEP offers annual awards to schools and districts for exemplary character education programs. On the Web site you can purchase materials, join the organization, and learn about conferences and workshops.

Ethics Resource Center
http://www.ethics.org

The Ethics Resource Center is a nonprofit, nonpartisan, educational organization whose vision is a world where individuals and organizations act with integrity. The mission of the Ethics Resource Center is to strengthen ethical leadership worldwide by providing leading-edge expertise and services through research, education, and partnerships.

Center for the Advancement of Ethics and Character
http://www.bu.edu/education/caec

The Web site for the Center for the Advancement of Ethics and Character at Boston University School of Education has sections for educators, parents, and students. It includes a manifesto with seven guiding principles, a complete character education reading list for all grade levels, and links to character education resources.

The Character Education Network
http://www.charactered.net

The Character Education Network provides parenting resources and character education curriculum and activities. The site is organized by nine of the most common character traits and is run exclusively in the United States by the National Center for Youth Issues, Inc. The center is a national, nonprofit organization that creates and supplies character education materials and training for schools, youth organizations, parents, and community groups.

Passkeys Foundation Jefferson Center for Character Education: Building a Nation of Character
http://www.jeffersoncenter.org

The Jefferson Center for Character Education teaches responsibility skills to America's kids. As a nonprofit, publicly supported foundation, Passkeys Foundation Jefferson Center for Character Education has been committed to building a nation of character for forty years. The Jefferson Center was founded in 1963, Passkeys Foundation was founded in 1978, and they merged in 2000. The Passkeys Jefferson Center now provides outstanding local and national character education programs for children, youth, and adults as well as markets character education curricula for K–8.

Character Development Group: The Spokes of Character Education
http://www.charactereducation.com

Dr. Philip Fitch Vincent, Director of the Character Development Group, brings more than twenty years of experience to his work in character education. The Web site includes concept guides—rules and procedures, cooperative learning, teaching for thinking, quality literature, and service learning. It also includes a wide variety of materials and workshops developed by Dr. Vincent.

Mahatma Gandhi on Character Education: Center for the 4th and 5th Rs: Respect and Responsibility
http://www.cortland.edu/c4n5rs

The Center for the 4th and 5th Rs serves as a regional, state, and national resource in character education, from the State University of New York College at Cortland. A growing national movement, character education is essential to the task of building a moral society and developing schools that are civil and caring communities. It includes a Twelve-Point Comprehensive Approach to Character Education, many resources, a newsletter edited by Dr. Thomas Lickona, information about conferences and institutes, and a Smart and Good High Schools Report.

Project Wisdom: Helping Students Make Wiser Choices
http://www.projectwisdom.com

Project Wisdom is an independent, nonpolitical, for-profit organization founded in 1992 by Leslie Luton Matula, an educator, community volunteer, and author. Project Wisdom provides a collection of daily words of wisdom to more than twelve thousand schools nationwide. These messages set a positive tone for the day by fostering ethical values and caring behavior. On the Web site you can read program evaluations and order the program and other free materials.

The Heartwood Institute
http://www.heartwoodethics.org

The Heartwood Institute teaches life lessons through literature-based character education for students from pre-K to grade 6. There are seven universal ethical attributes: courage, loyalty, justice, respect, hope, honesty, and love. Heartwood sells kits that provide teachers with everything needed to guide children in an exploration of universal, nonsectarian values within the core curriculum areas of literacy, social studies, and science. The lessons align with in language arts and social studies standards.

Institute for Global Ethics
http://www.globalethics.org

Founded in 1990, the Institute for Global Ethics is an independent, nonsectarian, nonpartisan, nonprofit organization dedicated to promoting ethical action in a global context. The challenge is to explore the global common ground of values, elevate awareness of ethics, and provide practical tools for making ethical decisions.

What Selection Criteria
Determined the Twelve Virtues?

We read and evaluated the resources on character education listed in the previous section, "What Sources Were Consulted?" A graph of the specific traits that were cited most often in the literature was prepared and examined.

We considered the availability of a wide range of fiction and nonfiction, from picture books to young adult, for each virtue. We then selected the virtues based on their years of experience working with literature and children.

A search was made for a few key people who would demonstrate these virtues and some broad subtopics that could be explored within each of these virtues.

The twelve virtues selected are empathy, respect, courage, humor, responsibility, perseverance, loyalty, honesty, cooperation, tolerance, citizenship, and forgiveness.

What Selection Criteria and Resources
Determined the Book Title Selection?

✧ Diversity

✧ Age levels covering all students from pre-K to grade 12

✧ Some nonfiction titles

✧ Some classic titles that would be found in most library collections

✧ Some recent titles

✧ Titles that would appeal to both girls and boys

✧ Character education Web sites (listed and described in this book)

✧ Character education resource books (listed and described in this book)

✧ Definitions of virtues are from www.dictionary.com

Because of space restrictions, we were unable to include everything we found. Often, the titles overlap with regard to the virtues they depict, but to balance our selections, we made a personal choice about where to place the title. Books were selected by the character trait portrayed and not necessarily by the subject matter. Therefore, some books for older readers are included and identified as such.

Chapter *1*

Empathy

Related Virtues

Compassion, consolation, caring, kindness, helpfulness, thoughtfulness, giving, sharing, sensitivity, appreciation, charity, concern, and generosity

Definition

Direct identification with, understanding of, and vicarious experience of another person's situation, feelings, and motives

Empathy in Action

- ✧ Be kind to new students.
- ✧ Share your supplies with those who have none.
- ✧ Care about your school work.
- ✧ Show appreciation to your teachers and coaches.
- ✧ Be polite in the cafeteria.
- ✧ Participate in community service projects initiated by your school.
- ✧ Remember the Golden Rule.
- ✧ Be kind to and understanding of older people.
- ✧ Be kind and helpful to those with mental and physical challenges.
- ✧ Be sensitive to the needs of others.

People Who Have Demonstrated This Virtue

- Gandhi
- Jimmy Carter
- Mother Teresa
- Princess Diana
- Dalai Lama
- Pearl Buck
- Jane Addams
- Swami Vivekananda
- Christopher Reeve
- Ida B. Wells

Organizations

- Habitat for Humanity
- World Hunger
- United Nations World Food Program
- United Nations International Children's Emergency Fund (UNICEF)
- American Association for Retired Persons (AARP)
- United Way
- American Red Cross
- Disabled American Veterans
- Humane Society of the United States
- American Society for the Prevention of Cruelty to Animals

Related Topics for Further Exploration

- Plight of homeless and hungry
- Origin of the USO Care Package
- Animal rescue organizations
- The plight of veterans
- The plight of the aged
- Americans adopting orphans

Discussion Questions

- How can you show compassion for others?
- What have you learned about people who care?
- How can you show people you care?
- Who is the most caring person you know?
- Which character in the book you read was a caring person? Was more than one character caring?
- Did any character in the book you read teach you something about caring or thoughtfulness?

✧ What does sensitivity mean to you?

✧ Do you use the Golden Rule?

Annotated Titles

Picture Books

Bunting. Eve. *Smoky Night*. Harcourt Children's Books, 1994. ISBN 0-15-269954-6
   This story is inspired by the Los Angeles riots of 1992. A young boy and his mother flee their apartment when it is set on fire. The boy worries about his missing cat and is pleased when a fireman brings his and a neighbor's cats to the shelter where they are staying. Before this night, the neighbor does not get along with the boy and his mother, nor do their cats like each other. But after the night of rioting, both the cats and their owners become friends. (ps–3)

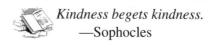

Kindness begets kindness.
—Sophocles

Caseley, Judith. *Bully*. Greenwillow Books, 2001. ISBN 0-688-17867-7
   Jack and Mickey are friends until Jack has a baby sister. Then Jack begins to bully Mickey. Mickey asks his family what he should do, and each member offers suggestions. Mickey follows everyone's advice: he is nice to Jack, uses brave words, brings him cookies, and makes him laugh. (ps–3)

Fox, Mem. *Wilfred Gordon McDonald Partridge*. Kanbe/Miller Books, 1995. ISBN 0-916-29156-1
   A boy lives next door to a nursing home in which several of his good friends reside. His likes Miss Nancy who has four names, just like he does; she is ninety-six years old and has trouble remembering things. Wilfred tries to help her. (K–3)

Myers, Christopher. *Wings*. Scholastic, 2000. ISBN 0-590-03377-8
   A new boy, Ikarus Jackson, starts school. Because he is different and has wings, the other children laugh and make fun of him. Ikarus leaves school and hovers overhead until a classmate finally tells him that his flying is beautiful. (1–3)

Pinkney, Jerry. *The Ugly Duckling*. Morrow Junior Books, 1999. ISBN 0-688-15932-X
   This is the traditional story of the ugly duckling that grows into the beautiful swan. The children recognize the new swan as the most beautiful of all the birds. The new swan realizes that even with the many hardships it experienced, the end result made it all worthwhile. Jerry Pinkney's illustrations are delightful. (K–4)

Ringgold, Faith. *The Invisible Princess*. Random House, 1998. ISBN 0-517-80024-1
   In this African American fairy tale set during the time of slavery, a baby princess is taken from her parents and raised by the Powers of Nature. Years pass and Patience, the daughter of the evil plantation owner, has a vision of a beautiful black girl playing in a field. The Invisible Princess eventually rescues her parents and the other slaves from their difficult lives. (0–3)

Primary (grades 1–3)

Calmenson, Stephanie. *Gator Halloween.* HarperCollins, 1999. ISBN 0-688-14785-2
　　Allie and Amy Gator want to create prize-winning Halloween costumes for the Swamp Street Halloween parade. They are trying to decide what to be when they see a poster for a missing pet lizard named Louie. They decide to find Louie and still try to make it to the parade in time. Even though they don't win the contest, they do find Louie, and there's a happy ending. (2–4)

Be pleasant until ten o'clock in the morning and the rest of the day will take care of itself.
　　—Elbert Hubbard

Howe, James. *Pinky and Rex and the Perfect Pumpkin.* Atheneum, 1998. ISBN 0-689-81782-7
　　Rex is invited to go to Pinky's grandparents' house to pick pumpkins. But Abby, Pinky's cousin, doesn't seem to want Rex to come along. Abby won't speak to Rex, makes fun of her, and doesn't include her in the activities. During the night, the special jack-o-lantern that grandfather carved is smashed. Who is the culprit? (1–3)

Keller, Holly. *A Bed Full of Cats.* Green Light Readers, 1999. ISBN 0-15-202262-7
　　Lee's cat, Flora, always sleeps on his bed. One night, she isn't there, and Lee's whole family helps him search for her. She is nowhere to be found. Then one night a few weeks later, Flora is back on his bed—with her new family of four kittens! (1–2)

Park, Barbara. *Junie B. Jones: First Grader (at last!)* Random House, 2001. ISBN 0-375-80293-2
　　Junie is finally a first grader, but she is in a new classroom with new kids and a new teacher. One familiar face, Lucille, is in her class, but things are not the same with her as they were last year. Next Junie gets glasses and worries that the kids will make fun of her. (1–3)

Pyle, Howard. *Bearskin.* Morrow Junior Books, 1997. ISBN 0-679-95101-6
　　The king is traveling through the countryside when the miller foretells that the baby crying in the next room will marry his daughter when he is older. The offended king takes the baby and gives him to the forester with instructions to kill him and bring back the heart as evidence. Instead, the forester packs the baby in a basket and sets it afloat. A bear finds the baby and raises "Bearskin" to adulthood. It prepares Bearskin for the world and the right to marry the princess. (K–4)

Waddell, Marilyn. *A Kitten Called Moonlight.* Candlewick Press, 2001. ISBN 0-7636-1176-X
　　Charlotte asks her mother to tell her yet again the story of Moonlight, a tiny abandoned kitten they find one cold, moonlit night. (ps–2)

Intermediate (grades 3–5)

Bauer, Marion Dane. *Runt.* Houghton Mifflin, 2002. ISBN 0-618-21261-2
　　In the forests of northern Minnesota, four healthy wolf pups are born, followed by one final small pup—the runt of the litter. "Runt" does a good job of keeping up with his siblings but is never able to please his father, the leader of the wolf pack. When he tries to capture a porcupine, kind humans find him and remove the painful quills from his muzzle. The porcupine eventually kills Runt's brother. Another wolf challenges the leader of the pack, and in the end it is Runt who rescues the pack and earns a new name. (3–up)

Creech, Sharon. *Love That Dog*. HarperCollins. 2001. ISBN 0-06-029287-3

Through the poems of a young boy, the story unfolds. The boy's yellow dog, Sky, chases a ball into the street, is hit by a car, and dies. Initially the boy resists poetry writing at school, but he eventually uses many famous poems and the inspiration of the poet Walter Dean Myers to help him write his own poem about Sky. (3–6)

DiCamillo, Kate. *Because of Winn Dixie*. Candlewick Press, 2000. ISBN 0-7636-0776-2

Opal moves with her father, a preacher, to Naomi, Florida. Opal is responsible for shopping at the local grocery store. At first, she doesn't see the dog, but when he creates a friendly commotion and the manager threatens to call the dog pound, Opal claims the dog is hers. When asked what the dog's name is, she responds, "Winn-Dixie," the name of the grocery store. Winn-Dixie, the dog, is a mutt who likes to smile using all of his teeth and has a pathological fear of thunderstorms. Winn-Dixie and Opal are responsible for soothing many lonely hearts in the town of Naomi. (4–6)

Kehret, Peg. *Don't Tell Anyone*. Dutton Children's Books, 2000. ISBN 0-525-46388-7

Megan discovers a group of feral cats living in a vacant lot. She brings them water and food everyday. One day she sees a sign saying that the lot will soon be cleared for a new apartment building. Megan attempts to save the cats and in the process gets involved with a desperate criminal. She is kidnapped and must find her way back to safety. (4–6)

Park, Barbara. *The Graduation of Jake Moon*. Atheneum Children's Books, 2000. ISBN 0-689-83912-X

Eighth-grader Jake and two of his friends let on that the old man is his grandfather, Skelly. Jake was always very close to his grandfather, and he doesn't know how to handle his Alzheimer's disease. As Jake reminisces about Skelly, he feels less guilty. Jake publicly acknowledges and rescues his grandfather at his eighth-grade graduation. (4–6)

Sachs, Marilyn. *The Four Ugly Cats in Apartment 3D*. Atheneum Children's Books, 2002. ISBN 0-689-84581-2

Lily lives in an apartment in San Francisco and has a good relationship with all of her neighbors except Mr. Freeman. One day Lily is locked out of her apartment after school, and she makes a lot of noise crying, disturbing Mr. Freeman. He invites her in, gives her milk and cookies, and introduces Lily to his four ugly cats. When Mr. Freeman suddenly dies, Lily tries to find good homes for each of the cats, but she has to do it within three days or the landlord will call the SPCA. (3–5)

Middle School (grades 5–8)

Adler, C. S. *More Than a Horse*. Clarion Books, 1997. ISBN 0-399-23627-9

Seventh-grader Leeann is upset about moving when her mother gets a better job as a cook at a dude ranch in Arizona. Once there, Leeann is actually pleased to be around so many horses, but on the first day, she makes the horse wrangler angry and is forbidden to be near the horses. She works hard to get back in the wrangler's good graces so that she can ride. She and friends from her new school eventually begin a riding program at the ranch for kids with special needs, and Leeann shows great compassion for the kids and the horses. (4–7)

Almond, David. *Skellig*. Delacorte, 1999. ISBN 0-385-32653-X

Michael's move to a new house and neighborhood is spoiled by his baby sister's serious illness. Michael's parents are constantly worried and preoccupied. Michael discovers a mysterious being named Skellig living in the garage. Michael and his new friend Mina help Skellig, and their relationship benefits everyone. (5–8)

Creech, Sharon. *Bloomability*. HarperCollins, 1998. ISBN 0-06-026993-6

Domenica Santolina Doone, or Dinnie, has lived in thirteen states in twelve years. Her parents suddenly send her to live in Lugano, Switzerland, with her Aunt Sandy and Uncle Max. Uncle Max is the headmaster at the American School and Dinnie finds herself learning to ski, learning Italian, and meeting other students from many different countries. (5–8)

Giff, Patricia Reilly. *Pictures of Hollis Woods*. Wendy Lamb Books (imprint of Random House Children's Books), 2002. ISBN 0-385-90070-8

Hollis Woods is a twelve-year-old girl who has spent her entire young life in foster homes. She finally seems to hit it off with Josie Cahill, a retired art teacher who lives on Long Island. Hollis sketches pictures of her former foster family, the Regans, whom she misses terribly. Eventually, Josie shows signs of aging, and Hollis becomes her caretaker. Hollis is loyal to Josie, gets help for her, and returns to the Regans for good. (4–7)

Holt, Kimberly Willis. *When Zachary Beaver Came to Town*. Henry Holt, 1999. ISBN 0-8050-6116-9

Tobey Wilson is thirteen years old and lives in a small Texas town. His mother left to become a country singer in Nashville. When Zachary Beaver, "The World's Fattest Boy," comes to town as part of a traveling sideshow, things begin to change for Tobey. Zachary is six hundred pounds and never leaves the trailer. Tobey eventually befriends him, but it isn't easy. Zachary is mean, rude, and a liar. (5–8)

 Forget injuries, never forget kindness.
—Confucius

Napoli, Donna Jo. *Three Days*. Dutton Children's Book, 2001. ISBN 0-525-46790-4

Jackie is kidnapped after her father dies from a heart attack while driving back to their hotel on a trip in Italy. Her captors keep Jackie for three days in an attempt to replace their daughter who recently died. Claudia, the mother of the deceased child, shows compassion and helps Jackie escape on a train to be reunited with her mother. (4–6)

Rylant, Cynthia. *Missing May*. Dell, 1992. ISBN 0-440-40865-2

For six years, Summer, age twelve, has lived with her Aunt May and Uncle Ob. They have shown her love and caring like she has never known before. Summer and Uncle Ob are devastated when Aunt May dies. Uncle Ob searches for someone to help him contact May to help get over the hurt. In the end, they know that they will always miss May but that they need to carry on and do their best. (5–8)

Spinelli, Jerry. *Wringer*. HarperCollins, 1977. ISBN 0-06-024913-7

Palmer LaRue receives "the treatment" when he is nine years old. It consists of nine hard ones with a knuckle on his left arm along with a new nickname, "Snots." The treatment is part of the town's tradition, along with Family Fest in August. The festival consists of a week of bumper cars, music, and cotton candy. It culminates on Saturday with Pigeon Day. On Pigeon Day, crates and crates of pigeons are brought into town. As the pigeons are released, and shooters take aim and fire. Those pigeons that are wounded or flopping around are put out of their misery by wringers. Palmer dreads his tenth birthday because he could be forced to be a wringer. Will he have the sensitivity to oppose tradition and his friend's expectations? (4–8)

YA (grades 8–12)

Brooks, Martha. *Being with Henry.* Dorling Kindersley, 2000. ISBN 0-7894-2588-2
Laker Wyatt's mother kicks him out of the house after he attacks stepfather number two, who verbally abuses her. Laker, age sixteen, takes a bus to another town and ends up panhandling to survive. An eighty-three-year-old man offers him a place to stay in exchange for yard work, and a friendship develops between them. (7–up)

Coman, Carolyn. *What Jamie Saw.* Front Street Press, 1995. ISBN 1-886910-02-2
Nine-year-old Jamie is awakened in the middle of the night and sees his stepfather throw his baby sister across the room. His mother appears at the doorway just in time to catch the baby. She puts the kids and their things in an old rusty car and drives away. Jamie's mother gets help from his teacher, and eventually they go to a place for battered families. The family begins life again in an old trailer far away from their old home. (6–9)

Curtis, Christopher Curtis. *Bucking the Sarge.* Wendy Lamb Books, 2004. ISBN: 0-440-41331-1
Luther T. Farrell and his mother, the Sarge, look at life differently. While the Sarge is after every buck she can get, regardless of who she hurts, Luther is just the opposite—he's kind, caring, and gentle. During school hours, Luther concentrates on trying to win the science fair for the third time. After school, fifteen-year-old Luther is in charge of the Happy Neighbor Group Home for Men. Luther's science project initiates an investigation by the mayor, which exposes Sarge's fraudulent practices. She gives Luther four days to find a new home. Luther looks at it as four days to plot his revenge against the Sarge. (8–up)

Levithan, David. *Are We There Yet?* Random House Children's Books, 2005. ISBN 0-375-82846
Two brothers, Danny and Elijah, have grown apart, but then they find themselves taking a trip to Rome and Florence, Italy, in place of their parents, who claim they are unable to go. They soon realize that this was a parental plan to help them grow closer. They have many adventures and different feelings, but in the end they realize the value of having a caring relationship. (YA)

Mikaelsen, Ben. *Petey.* Hyperion Books for Children, 1998. ISBN 0-7868-1336-9
Petey was born with cerebral palsy in the early 1920s, a time when doctors did not understand this condition. Everyone assumes Petey is an idiot, and so he is institutionalized. Because he is unable to speak, he wastes away in an asylum in Montana. His only contact is with a few occasional kind helpers who realize he is alert and certainly not retarded, only helpless in a deformed body. When Petey is in his seventies in a nursing home and some bullies are throwing snowballs at him, a young boy befriends him. The boy takes him out for walks, to the movies, and helps to get him a new and better wheelchair. (7–12)

Peck, Richard. *Strays Like Us.* Dial Books for Young Readers, 1998. ISBN 0-8037-2291-5
Twelve-year-old Molly, whose mother is a drug addict, is sent to live with her Great-Aunt Fay, a practical nurse. Molly discovers that Will, who lives next door, has been sent to his grandparents' to live. Molly is told that Will's dad is in jail but later discovers that he is dying of AIDS in the attic of the house. The family is afraid to let anyone know for fear of the town's negative reactions. Molly spends some time thinking that her mother will change and come for her, but eventually she realizes that she is fortunate to have Aunt Fay and that her home with her is permanent. (6–9)

Rylant, Cynthia. *Boris.* Harcourt Brace Jovanovich, 2005. ISBN 0-15-205412-X
Boris is a gray, humane-shelter cat who makes his way into the heart and home of a lady who enjoys his company and his style. The story is told in free verse and gives the reader an excellent description of Boris, whose former, and evidently well-deserved, name was Hunter. (YA)

Staples, Suzanne Fisher. *Haveli.* Random House, 1995. ISBN 0-679-86569-1

    In this sequel to *Shabanu,* the young Pakistani woman is the fourth wife of an elderly, powerful man, and together they have a five-year-old daughter. Shabanu, or daughter of the wind, is raised in the desert and is fiercely independent. She must now protect herself and her daughter from the older, spiteful, scheming wives, especially if her elderly husband dies. (6–9)

Strasser, Todd. *Can't Get There from Here.* Simon & Schuster, 2004. ISBN 0-689-84169-8

    A girl named Maybe lives on the streets of New York City with other homeless teens. Life is very difficult, and her friends are dying of hunger, disease, and drugs. A new girl, named Tears, joins the group, and Maybe decides to try to help her get off the streets before they all die. (YA)

_____. *Give a Boy a Gun.* Simon & Schuster, 2000. ISBN 0-689-81112-8

    This is the story of two boys, Gary Searle and Brendan Lawlor, who hold students hostage in a gym with automatic weapons and homemade bombs. Denise Shipley, Gary's stepsister, arrives home after the tragedy to interview friends, neighbors, teachers, and students to try to find out how and why this happened. Additional facts and statistics about guns and their usage are found throughout, set apart by a dotted line and smaller type. The author states in the Author's Note, "The story you are about to read is a work of fiction. Nothing—and everything—about it is real." (8-up)

 Flowers leave some of their fragrance in the hand that bestows them.
—Chinese Proverb

Zindel, Paul. *Loch: A Novel.* HarperCollins, 1994. ISBN 0-06-024542-5

    Loch accompanies his father, a famous oceanographer, and his sister Zaidee on an expedition to an isolated lake in Vermont. Loch's girlfriend, Sarah, also comes along. They find a family of prehistoric plesiosaurs, trapped in the lake by a salmon grid that keeps them from going into the deeper waters of Lake Champlain. Loch, Zaidee, and Sarah help the plesiosaurs to escape the death planned for them by Cavenger, Sarah's father and the financier of the expedition. (6–9)

Nonfiction

Fradin, Dennis, and Judith. *Ida B. Wells: Mother of the Civil Rights Movement.* Houghton Mifflin, 2000. ISBN 0-395-89898-6

    This is the biography of an inspiring woman who was born a slave and became a teacher, probation officer, journalist, and activist. She fought for black women to gain the right to vote and worked hard to stop the horrible practice of lynching. She also helped to create the National Association for the Advancement of Colored People. (5–up)

Josephson, Judith Pinkerton. *Mother Jones: Fierce Fighter for Workers' Rights.* Lerner, 1997. ISBN 0-8225-4924-7

    This is biography of the determined Mother Jones who organized labor rights—specifically, the conditions in mines. (6–up)

Middleton, Haydn. *Diana Princess of Wales.* Heinemann Library, 1999. ISBN 1-57572-715-3

    Born into the upper English class, Diana married Prince Charles, the heir to the throne, in 1981. The public grew to love the shy Diana and was charmed by her open, loving ways, so different from the other members of the royal family. She was expected to carry out a number of duties, and she concentrated on helping those with AIDS and leprosy, as well as the less fortunate and neglected. She supported the work of the Red Cross and drew global attention to the effects of land-mine accidents. Diana once said, "I'm not a political animal, but I think the biggest disease this world suffers from in this day and age is the disease of feeling unloved." (0–2)

————. *Mother Teresa*. Heinemann Library, 2000. ISBN 1-57572-227-5

One of the world's great humanitarians and winner of the Nobel Peace Prize in 1979, Mother Teresa of Calcutta, devoted her life to helping the poor of India and other countries. (4–6)

Mochizuki, Ken. *Passage to Freedom: The Sugihara Story*. Lee & Low Books, 1997. ISBN 1-880000-49-0

Passage to Freedom is told from the son's point of view about his father, who was a Japanese diplomat in Poland just before World War II. One morning, a crowd of Jews from Poland lined up in front of their house asking for visas to go to Japan. For one month, the boy's father disobeyed his superiors and issued visas by hand to the Polish Jews until he was forced to leave his home because of the approaching Russians and Germans. (3–5)

Chapter 2

Respect

Related Virtues

Courtesy, manners, politeness, honor, admiration, and appreciation

Definition

A feeling of appreciative, often deferential regard; esteem

Respect in Action

- ✧ Respect your teachers and coaches.
- ✧ Respect your classmates.
- ✧ Respect yourself.
- ✧ Respect the police and people of authority.
- ✧ Respect the Earth.
- ✧ Respect others on the Internet.
- ✧ Show respect by promoting recycling.
- ✧ Abide by your school's honor code.
- ✧ Do not cheat.
- ✧ Respect your school's facilities.
- ✧ Respect the belongings of your classmates.
- ✧ Show courtesy to everyone at school.
- ✧ Greet all adults appropriately by name.
- ✧ Hold doors open for others.
- ✧ Say please and thank you.

People Who Have Demonstrated This Virtue

- ✧ Martin Luther King, Jr.
- ✧ Walt Disney
- ✧ Hillel
- ✧ Rosalynn Carter
- ✧ Arthur Ashe
- ✧ Jackie Robinson
- ✧ Joseph Pulitzer
- ✧ Langston Hughes
- ✧ Robert Frost

Related Topics for Further Exploration

- ✧ Manners and etiquette
- ✧ Netiquette
- ✧ Politically correct
- ✧ History of table manners
- ✧ Customs of other countries that demonstrate respect
- ✧ Emily Post and manners
- ✧ Japanese tea ceremony
- ✧ Flag etiquette
- ✧ Boat/ship etiquette
- ✧ Nobel Prizes

Discussion Questions

- ✧ Who are the people in positions of authority in your life?
- ✧ Who are the elders that you can learn from?
- ✧ Why are table manners important?
- ✧ Why is gossip disrespectful?
- ✧ How can you show respect for the earth?
- ✧ Why is it important to show respect for animals?
- ✧ Why is it important to stand up for others?
- ✧ What are some examples of self-respect?

Annotated Titles

Picture Books

Bottner, Barbara. *Bootsie Barker Bites.* G. P. Putnam's Sons, 1992. ISBN 0-399-22125-5
    The timid narrator is tortured by her frequent visitor, Bootsie Barker, who pulls her hair and doesn't like the narrator's pet salamander. So when Bootsie is planning on staying the weekend, the narrator thinks of a new game to play that will make Bootsie leave immediately. (K–3)

Bunting, Eve. *Butterfly House.* Scholastic, 1999. ISBN 0590-84884-4
    A little girl saves a larva from being eaten by a hungry blue jay. With the help of her grandfather, she makes a colorful garden home for the larva and watches its transformation into a butterfly. Many years later, in the spring when the young girl is now much older, many butterflies, called "painted ladies," flock to her flowers and return the love she gave so many years ago. (K–3)

Choldenko, Gennifer. *Moonstruck: The True Story of the Cow Who Jumped over the Moon.* Hyperion Books for Children, 1997. ISBN 0-7868-0158-1
    An old brown horse tells the story, starting with a complaint to Mother Goose that the cow deserved much more than one line in the poem. The horse then says that horses have always jumped over the moon, and they train long and hard to be able to do so. Then one day a cow shows up and wants to train, too. And train she does. She really earns the respect of all the horses when she finally succeeds and jumps over the moon. (K–2)

Curtis, Jamie Lee. *I'm Gonna Like Me: Letting Off a Little Self-Esteem.* HarperCollins, 2002. ISBN 0-06-028762-4
    A little boy and girl describe themselves in alternating situations where they like themselves no matter what. "I'm gonna like me 'cause I'm loved and I know it, and liking myself is the best way to show it." (ps–3)

Johnston, Tony. *Cat, What Is That?* HarperCollins, 2001. ISBN 0-0602-7742-4
    Beautiful illustrations and compact verse show cats in all sorts of poses. The cats show off their regal stance, grace, sophistication, and subtle personalities. (K–4)

Kilborne, Sarah. *Peach & Blue.* Alfred A. Knopf Books for Young Readers, 1994. ISBN 0-679-83929-1
    This is an unusual tale of a blue-bellied frog who befriends a sad peach high in a tree. The peach is sad because she will never see the world, so the frog takes her from the branch and shows her the life around the pond, pointing out all the beauty in nature. There is much mutual respect in this strange friendship, with the frog doing everything he can to make the peach comfortable. (K–2)

Meddaugh, Susan. *Martha and Skits.* Houghton Mifflin, 2000. ISBN 0-618-05776-5
    Martha, the talking dog, has a life-changing experience when the family adopts a new brown puppy named Skits. The puppy chews on everything in sight and gets into normal puppy trouble. He envies Martha's ability to talk and wants to do the same when he grows up. Martha is quick to help him discover where *his* talent lies—in catching flying objects. (ps–3)

Pilkey, Dav. *The Hallo-Wiener.* Scholastic, 1995. ISBN 0-590-41703-7
    Oscar is longer than he is tall. His friends make fun of him and call him a wiener dog. On Halloween, his mother makes him a costume, a giant hot-dog bun. Oscar does not want to hurt

his mother's feelings, so he wears the costume and his friends make even more fun of him. Oscar saves his friends from an embarrassing situation, and they declare him a "Hero Sandwich." (K–3)

Say, Allen. *Emma's Rug.* Houghton Mifflin, 1996. ISBN 0-395-74294-3
        A small rug is placed beside Emma's crib when she is a baby. She never stands on the rug but stares at it for a very long time. Later when she begins to draw and paint, she is asked where she receives her ideas. Emma replies that she just copies. One day Emma's mother takes the rug and washes it. Emma is distraught and she throws all of her paint supplies and medals in the trash. When she goes back to her room, she is surprised when once again she sees images begging to be painted. (1–3)

A good friend who points out mistakes and imperfections and rebukes evil is to be respected as if he reveals a secret of hidden treasure.
—Buddha

Schanzer, Rosalyn. *Davy Crockett Saves the World.* HarperCollins, 2001. ISBN 0-688-16991-0
        This tall tale tells how Davy Crockett was asked by the president of the United States to save the world by pulling the tail off of Halley's Comet. Davy does such a good job, he is able to marry Sally Sugartree and is elected to Congress. (K–3)

Willems, Mo. *Time to Say "Please"!* Hyperion Books for Children, 2005. ISBN 0-7868-5293-3
        Situations are graphically demonstrated to show when you should say "please," "excuse me," "sorry" ("but you have to mean it!"), and "thank you." The book includes a board game. (ps–1)

Wood, Audrey. *Rude Giants.* Harcourt Brace Jovanovich, 1993. ISBN 0-15-269412-9
        Beatrix and her cow, Gerda, have an ideal life until two rude giants move into an empty castle on the hill. Beatrix demonstrates what good manners mean. (ps–2)

Young, Ed. *Night Visitors.* Philomel, 1995. ISBN 0399-22731-8
        Ants invade the family's rice storehouse, so Ho Kuan's father wants to trace the ants to their nest and drown them. Ho asks his father to give him a month to seal the walls and floor so tight that no ant will enter. Ho respects all forms of life, no matter how small. (ps–3)

Primary (grades 1–3)

Brett, Jan. *Beauty and the Beast.* Clarion Books, 1989. ISBN 0-89919-497-4
        A beautifully illustrated telling of the classic tale of the "Beauty and the Beast." When Beauty's father plucks a rose for his daughter, the aroused Beast allows him to leave as long as one of his daughters willingly returns. In time, Beauty grows to love the Beast, and after she mistakenly thinks she has lost him for good, she agrees to marry him. Her tears, respect, and promise of love break the spell at the palace, and the Beast turns into a handsome young man. Together they live happily ever after. (0–3)

Christopher, Matt. *Secret Weapon.* Little, Brown and Company, 2000. ISBN 0-316-13458-9
        This story combines good sportsmanship, soccer, and strong family values. Lisa is self-conscious because she is small and has trouble making a throw-in. Her coach finds out that she

is gymnastically inclined, so he encourages her to work on a secret weapon—a flip throw that will help her win points for the team. (2–4)

Fleischman, Paul. *Weslandia.* Candlewick Press, 1999. ISBN 0-7636-0006-7

Wesley is a nerd, a boy who spends his time running from kids who tease and torment him. He decides to spend his summer vacation building his own civilization. He discovers a new plant, which provides him with food, clothes, and suntan oil. He creates a new alphabet, a number system, and new sports. His tormentors are curious about all this and become his friends and followers. (K–4)

Greene, Stephanie. *Owen Foote, Second Grade Strongman.* Clarion Books, 1996. ISBN 0-395-72098-2

Owen is in second grade and embarrassed by his small size. He confides in his friend, Joseph, and finds that he, too, is embarrassed—but about being overweight. They are both very apprehensive about being humiliated by the school nurse, Mrs. Jackson, on height and weight chart day. When the day comes, Owen tells Mrs. Jackson to speak quietly and is immediately in trouble with the principal and his parents until he apologizes. (1–3)

Hamm, Mia. *Winners Never Quit.* HarperCollins, 2004. ISBN 0-06-074-0507

Mia Hamm learns how to lose gracefully when she plays soccer with her family. She does not like to lose, but she loves playing soccer more because "winners never quit." (ps–2)

Lester, Julius. *Black Cowboy, Wild Horses: A True Story.* Dial Books for Young Readers, 1998. ISBN 0-8037-1787-3

This story is based on an incident in the life of the black cowboy, Bob Lemmons, who has an uncanny knack for tracking. He finds a herd of wild stallions and eventually joins them on his horse, Warrior, and then challenges and wins control of the herd from the lead stallion. He then brings the herd of wild mustangs back to the ranch corral. (2–4)

Rylant, Cynthia. *Special Gifts.* Aladdin Paperbacks, 2000. ISBN 0-689-81715-0

Lily, Rosie, and Tess are cousins who live with their Aunt Lucy while their parents travel the world. The girls are nine years old, and they share an attic in Aunt Lucy's big, old house. In this book in the Cobble Street Cousins series, the girls are off from school for three weeks, and they decide to learn how to sew. (3–6)

Schnetzler, Pattie. *Earth Day Birthday.* Dawn Publications, 2003. ISBN 1-58469-054-2

This beautifully illustrated book has an environmental theme that can be sung to the *Twelve Days of Christmas.* It also includes some suggestions on ways to celebrate Earth Day. (ps–4)

Intermediate (grades 3–5)

Cutler, Jane. *'Gator Aid.* Farrar, Straus & Giroux, 1999. ISBN 0-374-42521-3

Edward is in the second grade, and rumors fly when he tells people he has seen a baby alligator in the local public park. (3–5)

Gutman. Dan. *Jackie and Me: A Baseball Card Adventure.* HarperCollins, 1999. ISBN 0-380-97685-4

At school, Joe Stoshack is assigned a report on a famous African American who has made a contribution to society. Joe uses baseball cards to travel back in time and selects the Jackie Robinson card. He travels back to the 1940s to get a firsthand impression of what it was like to be black and to break the color barrier in major league baseball. (4–7)

Haddix, Margaret Peterson. *Say What?* Simon & Schuster, 2004. ISBN 0-689-86256-3

Mom and dad think their kids no longer listen to what they say, so they try an experiment. Every time Sukie and her two older brothers do something wrong, the parents say something that has nothing to do with the situation. The kids are baffled—why don't their parents yell like they used to? When the kids find out about their parents' "plan," they retaliate with a plan of their own. Soon parents and children are speaking to each other in complete nonsense. Eventually the family agrees to go back to normal with both the kids and adults trying harder not to fall into familiar patterns. (2–4)

 Civilization is a method of living, an attitude of equal respect for all men.
—Jane Addams

McKay, Hilary. *The Amber Cat.* Margaret K. McElderry Books, 1997. ISBN 0-689-81360-0

Robin Brogan, his friend Dan, and his neighbor Sun Dance are all sick with the chicken pox. Mrs. Brogan tells them a story from when she was eleven years old about a stranger named Harriet who would come and go. Somehow, Harriet seems to give an amber cat to Sun Dance, and Mrs. Brogan recognizes the cat as the one Harriet gave to her friend Charley long ago. (4–6)

Myers, Laurie. *Surviving Brick Johnson.* Clarion Books, 2000. ISBN 0-395-98031-3

Alex was in the lunchroom doing imitations when he does an imitation of Brick Johnson, a new student in school. Brick sees Alex doing the imitation, and he says what he did to a boy who did the same thing in his old school, but he never finishes his statement. From that moment on, Alex begins to worry about how Brick will retaliate. Alex takes karate lessons in self-defense and at his second lesson, Brick Johnson also starts in the same class for the same reason. With help from his little brother, Alex realizes that Brick is not a bully. (3–5)

Pinkwater, Daniel. *Fat Camp Commandos Go West.* Scholastic, 2002. ISBN 0-439-29772-9

Sylvia and Ralph are being sent to Camp Noo Yoo, a fat camp, for the second time. They hate it and leave when they have the opportunity to spend the rest of the summer with Mavis Goldfarb. Mavis's parents are away, so they go to her house and set into operation a campaign to end prejudice against fat people. (3–8)

Scieszka, Jon. *Summer Reading Is Killing Me.* Viking, 1998. ISBN 0-670-880411-8

Sam, Fred, and Joe—the Time Warp Trio—are off on another adventure. This time Fred puts their summer reading list in the magic book that transports them to a different time. Now their summer reading stories are all mixed up together, causing a huge nightmare. They must find the magic book and remove the list before all the good characters are killed off by the bad characters. (3–6)

Van Draanen, Wendelin. *Sammy Keyes and the Sisters of Mercy.* Knopf, 1999. ISBN 0-679-88852-7

Seventh-grader Sammy Keyes is working off twenty hours of detention time at St. Mary's Church after school. Father Mayhew's cross is stolen, and Sammy becomes the prime suspect. She puts all her sleuthing skills to work and uncovers a huge heist. At the same time, she plays on a softball team that is in the playoffs and deals with dirty tricks played on her by her rival, Heather. (4–7)

Voigt, Cynthia. *Bad Girls.* Scholastic, 1996. ISBN 0-590-601341-2

Two fifth graders, Mickey and Margalo, are both new students and have a knack for stirring up trouble. Mickey is noisy and pushy, and Margalo is quiet and sneaky. When Margalo's pranks catch up to her and she gets in trouble, Mickey stands by her side. They demand respect from their classmates because of their hilarious, attention-getting antics. (4–6)

Wittlinger, Ellen. *Gracie's Girl.* Aladdin, 2002. ISBN 0-689-84960-5

Bess is entering middle school, and in an attempt to be cool, she frequents thrift shops looking for different clothes. This is where she first meets Gracie, a homeless elderly woman who eats out of the garbage and sleeps on the street. Later, Bess meets Gracie at the homeless shelter where she is helping to serve Sunday dinner. Bess has typical middle school problems, but they become less important as she tries to find food and shelter for Gracie. (4–6)

Wright, Betty Ren. *The Ghost in Room 11.* Holiday House, 1998. ISBN 0-8234-1318-7

Matt Barber is having trouble making friends in his new school. He tries to impress his classmates by telling tall tales about his parents, so when he says that he has seen a ghost roaming outside room 11 in the school, no one believes him. (2–6)

Middle School (grades 5–8)

Eckert, Allan. *Return to Hawk's Hill.* Little, Brown & Company, 1998. ISBN 0-316-00689-0

In a story set in northern Canada in the 1870s, seven-year-old Ben MacDonald runs from a vicious trapper and jumps into a boat and drifts down the river. A young hunter from the Cree tribe rescues him and takes him to the tribes' settlement. Ben's father and brother search for him, fearing that the trapper has done something to him. Ben surprises and delights the members of the tribe with his ability to communicate with wild animals. Ben and his family are finally reunited, and the mean trapper is run off for good. (5–7)

Fletcher, Susan. *Walk Across the Sea.* Atheneum Children's Books, 2001. ISBN 0-689-84133-7

In the 1880s, Eliza Jane McCully lives with her family in a lighthouse on the coast of northern California. At this time, Chinese immigrant workers were being expelled from California. One day a boy named Wah Chung saves Eliza from a big wave, and Eliza must take a closer look at her feelings about the Chinese. When the townspeople are forcibly evicting the Chinese from their homes, Eliza hides Wah Chung in the lighthouse, and in the end this causes her father to lose his job as the lighthouse keeper. (5–9)

Gray, Luli. *Falcon and the Charles Street Witch.* Houghton Mifflin, 2002. ISBN 0-618-16410-3

In this sequel to *Falcon's Egg*, the heroine, Falcon, is in search of her younger brother who has accidentally fallen out of a jumbo jet. She leaps out to save him and ends up at the home of a witch who helps her find her brother. (4–6)

Hoobler, Dorothy. *The Ghost in the Tokaido Inn.* Philomel, 1999. ISBN 0-399-23330-X

In eighteenth-century Japan, fourteen-year-old Seikei is the son of a tea merchant, but he wants to be a samurai. The problem is that one can't just become a samurai; you must be born into it. While on a business trip with his father, he witnesses the theft of a costly jewel from an arrogant samurai. The famous magistrate, Judge Ooka, asks Seikei to help him find the thief, and this leads him into the world of Kabuki theater. (6–8)

Kinsey-Warnock, Natalie. *As Long as There Are Mountains.* Cobblehill/Dutton, 1997. ISBN 0-525-652361

Iris Anderson, thirteen years old, takes great pleasure in her family farm in Vermont. Her older brother, Lucien, has no interest in the farm and wants to go to college and become a writer. Someone burns down the barn, and her father, Hazen, has a serious accident that leaves him depressed. Hazen's brother-in-law helps to save the farm. Iris shows great respect for the land and wants the farm to be hers someday. (4–7)

Myers, Walter Dean. *The Journal of Scott Pendleton Collins.* Scholastic, 1999. ISBN 0-439-05013-8

> Scott Collins is five weeks away from D-Day when the journal begins. After the event, he is a survivor, and the novel ends with Scott waiting to cross the English Channel after being wounded in France. (5–8)

Schur, Maxine. *The Circlemaker.* Dial Books for Young Readers, 1994. ISBN 0-8037-1354-1

> In 1852, Czar Nicholas sends soldiers to a small Ukrainian town looking for Jewish boys for the army. Twelve-year-old Mendel runs away and joins Dovid, an abusive bully who has just escaped from the army, and they make their way to freedom. (5–7)

Smith, Roland. *Thunder Cave.* Hyperion Books for Young Readers, 1995. ISBN 0-7868-0068-2

> This ecological adventure story is about fourteen-year-old Jake who goes to Kenya in search of his father, a wildlife biologist, after his mother has been hit and killed by a car while jogging. In the process of finding his father, Jake is mugged and befriends a young Masai. Together they meet up with a group of poachers. (5–8)

YA (grades 8–12)

Brooks, Bruce. *All That Remains.* Atheneum Books for Young Readers, 2001. ISBN 0-689-83351-2

> This is a trilogy of stories where the main characters must deal with the remains of a deceased loved one. In one, cousins plan to keep their aunt who died of AIDS out of a pauper's cemetery, where she would be buried as required by state laws. In another, a very cool teenager promises his dying uncle that he will take care of his nerdy cousin, the uncle's son. In the last story, a girl carrying a backpack with her father's remains challenges some boys to a round of golf. (7–up)

Conford, Ellen. *Crush.* HarperCollins, 1998. ISBN 0-06-025414-9

> Ten interrelated stories about a group of high school students before the Valentine's dance called the Sweetheart Stomp. (5–8)

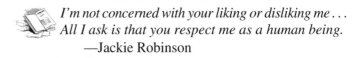

> *I'm not concerned with your liking or disliking me . . .*
> *All I ask is that you respect me as a human being.*
> —Jackie Robinson

Cooney, Caroline B. *Flash Fire.* Scholastic, 1995. ISBN 0-590-25253-4

> Fifteen year old, Danna Press watches the wildfires burning out of control in Los Angeles. They reach her community and she tries to fight the fire, but eventually she has to leave with her brother. The whole story takes place in under two hours and is filled with information about fires and firefighting. (6–8)

Cormier, Robert. *Tenderness.* Delacorte Press, 1997. ISBN 0-385-32286-0

> Eighteen-year-old Eric Poole is released after three years in juvenile detention for the murder of his mother and stepfather. Lieutenant Jake Proctor thinks Eric is responsible for the unsolved murders of two girls. Eric meets a fifteen-year-old runaway named Lori, and she helps him to keep away from Proctor but ends up ensuring his conviction when she dies by accident. (6–up)

Dessen, Sarah. *Dreamland.* Viking, 2000. ISBN 0-670-89122-3

> Caitlin's older sister, Cass, left home with her boyfriend just before Cass starts her freshman year at Yale. Caitlin thinks Cass is perfect and feels she can never live up to Cass's reputation. Now Cass is gone, and Caitlin must find her own way. Caitlin meets Rogerson and gradually succumbs to a dreamlike existence. She becomes more dependent on Rogerson as he asserts

control over and physically abuses her. Caitlin is losing her self-respect and needs help fast. (9–up)

Howarth, Lesley. *MapHead: The Return.* Candlewick, 1997. ISBN 1-56402-416-4
This is a sequel featuring a boy from a parallel universe named MapHead, so called because he can show maps on his bald head. He befriends a boy named Jack Stamp and goes to stay with Jack's family. He invades Jack's mind, and, as a result, Jack gets into all kinds of trouble. MapHead has to change his ways and tries to show his love and concern for Jack's family. (8–10)

Kim, Helen. *The Long Season of Rain.* Henry Holt, 1996. ISBN 0-8050-4758-1
This story takes place in Seoul, Korea, in the summer of 1969. It is told from the point of view of Junehee, the second of four sisters. The story is about her mother who moves into the mother-in-law's house and consequently has no rights. Her domineering husband is away much of the time and is unfaithful to his wife. When the family takes in an orphaned boy, Junehee and her mother befriend him. Her mother wishes to adopt him, but her husband and mother-in-law forbid it; to their surprise, the mother leaves. (7–up)

Kingsolver, Barbara. *The Poisonwood Bible.* Harper Trade, 1998. ISBN 0-06-093053-5
This novel spans thirty years and is told in alternating chapters from the point of view of the women in this story. Nathan Price, an evangelical minister, uproots his wife and four daughters; they move from Georgia to the Belgian Congo in the late 1950s. Nathan is a fanatic, culturally unaware, and emotionally abusive. Each of the women tells her own story and the effect Africa has on them. (General Adult)

Koertge, Ronald. *Stoner & Spaz.* Candlewick Press, 2002. ISBN 0-7636-1608-7
Sixteen-year-old Ben Bancroft has cerebral palsy and lives with his wealthy, overprotective grandmother. He is a loner who is addicted to old movies. Colleen Minou is always high, her clothes are from the Salvation Army, she is tattooed everywhere, and she has a foul mouth. They become a couple—she is the first person who ever really noticed Ben and who actually teases him about his disability. She takes him to clubs, gives him his first joint, and actually challenges him to direct his own movie. He challenges her to get off the drugs, but she is unable to do so. What will happen to Ben, who is seriously addicted to Colleen? (9–up)

Laird, Christa. *But Can the Phoenix Sing?* Greenwillow Books, 1993. ISBN 0-688-13612-5
Misha Edelman leaves a letter to his alienated stepson explaining his life during the war, his escape from the Warsaw ghetto, his life as a partisan fighter, and his work as a courier. Misha hopes that he can establish a relationship once his stepson understands him and why he acts the way he does. (7–up)

Lynch, Chris. *Extreme Elvin.* HarperCollins, 1999. ISBN 0-06-028040-9
Overweight Elvin is a freshman at a boy's Catholic high school and experiences the ups and downs of being fourteen. (8–10)

_____. *Slot Machine.* HarperCollins, 1995. ISBN 0-06-447140-3
The camp is called Twenty-One Nights with the Knights, and it is a three-week-long summer camp for freshmen at an all-male Catholic high school. Fourteen-year-old Elvin Bishop is overweight and lazy—and definitely not interested in any of the sports planned at the camp. His friends find their athletic slots with relative ease while Elvin bounces from one humiliating attempt at a sport to another. He would like to fit in somewhere but does not want to lose his self-respect to do so. (7–10)

Powell, Randy. *Dean Duffy.* Farrar, Straus & Giroux, 1995. ISBN 0-374-31754-2

>   Eighteen-year-old Dean Duffy was once a great baseball player. From Little League to his freshman year of high school, he was a star. But then he couldn't pitch; next, he couldn't hit. By the time he should have been selecting his college baseball scholarship, no one was interested in him. An adult friend gets him a trial scholarship at a private college for the next spring, and Dean has to decide what he will do. (7–up)

Rees, Celia. *Witch Child.* Candlewick Press, 2001. ISBN 0-7636-1421-1

>   The journal of Mary Newbury, written in 1659, begins with her stating that she is a witch. She sees her grandmother hung as a witch in her English village. Mary is placed onboard a ship heading to America. Mary finds a new family and friends there, but as in England, witches are blamed for everything wrong that happens. Mary and a few friends retreat to the forest, but the climate of fear and blame are all-encompassing. (5–9)

It is not desirable to cultivate a respect for law, so much as a respect for right.
—Henry David Thoreau

Yolen, Jane, and Richard J. Harris. *Girl in a Cage.* Philomel Books, 2002. ISBN 0-399-23627-9

>   Robert Bruce, king of Scotland, is able to keep away from his enemy, Edward I of England. But Bruce's eleven-year-old daughter, Marjorie, gets captured and is taken to a small English village and locked in an outdoor iron cage. Marjorie is teased and ridiculed by the townspeople. In dealing with her imprisonment, Marjorie shows tremendous self-respect. (6–10)

Nonfiction

MacGregor, Cynthia. *Think for Yourself: A Kid's Guide to Solving Life's Dilemmas and Other Sticky Problems.* Lobster Press, 2003. ISBN 1-894222-73-3

>   The author gives examples of common situations that kids face and suggestions on how to solve them. The examples include problems with manners, moral problems, and a combination of both manners and morals. (4–7)

Martin, Marvin. *Arthur Ashe: Of Tennis and the Human Spirit.* Franklin Watts, 1999. ISBN 0-531-11432-5

>   Arthur Ashe was the first African American to play professional tennis. He had to stand up to bigotry and racial prejudice. He was respected both on and off the court. He helped establish the National Junior Tennis League and was a leader in the struggle against apartheid in South Africa. "Arthur Ashe wanted all the races of the world to live together in peace and harmony." (6–9)

Rummel, Jack. *Langston Hughes: Poet.* Chelsea House, 1988. ISBN 1-555-46595-1

>   Langston Hughes was a leading black American poet. When he graduated from high school, he found work in Mexico teaching English in a private school. He sent three poems to a new magazine for black children, and one was accepted. Once his father saw his success, he offered to pay for his first year at Columbia if he would study engineering. After one year, Langston decided he wanted to write poetry and left school. Hughes traveled a great deal, and his poetry incorporates black music and speech. (6–12)

Selden, Bernice. *The Story of Walt Disney: Maker of Magical Worlds.* Bantam Doubleday Dell Books for Young Readers, 1989. ISBN 0-440-402409

Walt Disney created a magical world for children in spite of the fact that his own childhood was not very happy. Walt Disney is known throughout the world as the creator of Mickey Mouse, Donald Duck, Disney World, Disneyland, and numerous films. (4–7)

Swain, Gwenyth. *Johnny Appleseed.* Carolrhoda, 2001. ISBN 1-57505-519-8

This is an easy-to-read biography about Johnny Appleseed. As a young man he went to Pennsylvania and began to plant apple trees. When the settlers moved into Pennsylvania, Johnny sold or traded his apple trees. As the land was settled, Johnny continued to move west planting his apple seeds and the word of God. (1–2)

Chapter 3

Courage

Related Virtues

Bravery, spirit, tenacity, resolve, daring, and boldness

Definition

The state or quality of mind or spirit that enables one to face danger, fear, or vicissitudes with self-possession, confidence, and resolution; bravery

Courage in Action

⬦ Stand up for your beliefs.

⬦ Do not join in when others are doing something wrong.

⬦ Defend those who can't defend themselves.

⬦ Practice virtuous behaviors.

⬦ Do not participate in any type of bullying.

⬦ Invite new students to join you at lunch.

People Who Have Demonstrated This Virtue

⬦ Rosa Parks

⬦ Harriet Tubman

⬦ Anne Frank

⬦ Thomas Edison

⬦ Admiral Richard E. Byrd

⬦ Eleanor Roosevelt

Related Topics for Further Exploration

- *Red Badge of Courage* by Stephen Crane
- *Apollo 13*
- Test of courage—men and women learning to become firefighters
- Lions as symbols of courage
- *Braveheart*
- The Underground Railroad
- Physically challenged
- Explorers and conquerors
- History of the Civil Rights Movement
- Soldiers and bravery in war
- Phobias

Discussion Questions

- What makes a hero?
- What do you think of when you hear the word hero?
- Are heroes always famous people?
- How did the characters demonstrate courage in the book you read?
- Does peer pressure influence courageous behavior?
- How can you be courageous in your own life?
- How do you overcome fear of something?
- What are convictions? Give some examples.

Annotated Titles

Picture Books

Cocca-Leffler, Maryann. *Bravery Soup.* Albert Whitman, 2002. ISBN 0-8075-0870-5
     Carlin is afraid of most everything, so he asks Big Bear what he can do. Big Bear tells Carlin that he must go alone through the Forbidden Forest to Skulk Mountain and assures him that he is braver than he thinks he is. Carlin disposes of all the gifts his friends give him and makes his way to Skulk Mountain. After facing the monster, he grabs the box and quickly leaves. When he gets back to Big Bear, Carlin discovers the box is empty. Big Bear knows this, and reminds Carlin that it is not what is in the box but what is inside of Carlin that makes him brave and courageous. (ps–2)

Edwards, Pamela Duncan. *Clara Caterpillar.* HarperCollins, 2001. ISBN 0-06-028996-1
     Clara is a common cabbage caterpillar who will become a common cabbage butterfly. She is cream colored, but she will come to the rescue of the more colorful butterflies. She will distract the crow and then camouflage herself among the cream-colored camellias. The other butterflies realize how courageous Clara is and vow to stay close to the common cabbage butterfly. (K–3)

Ernst, Lisa Campbell. *Ginger Jumps.* Bradbury Press, 1990. ISBN 0-02-733565-8

Ginger is a circus dog who dreams about a young girl who will play with her and love her. A new act is introduced in the circus, and they need a hardworking dog in the act. Ginger is picked, and she begins practicing on stairs and a trampoline. But when she sees the height she is expected to jump from, she can't do it. Ginger is discouraged until she sees the new act: the little girl she had been hoping for. When it is time for a dog to jump from the high stairs into the arms of the little girl, Ginger is ready. (ps–02)

Graham, Bob. *Max.* Candlewick Press, 2000. ISBN 0-7636-1138-7

Will Max grow up to be a superhero like his mom, Madam Thunderbolt, and his dad, Captain Lightning? Max is a super baby who does not fly until the day he rescues a baby bird that falls from its nest. Then he becomes a "small hero doing quiet deeds." (ps–1)

Henkes, Kevin. *Sheila Rae, the Brave.* Greenwillow Books, 1987. ISBN 0-688-07155-4

Sheila Rae is a brave mouse. She does many things to prove to everyone that she has self-confidence. One day she decides to take a new way home from school, and she gets lost and frightened. Luckily, her little sister Louise was sneaking along behind her, and together they find their way back home. Sheila Rae no longer teases Louise about being a scaredy cat. (ps–3)

Khan, Rukhsana. *Ruler of the Courtyard.* Viking, 2003. ISBN 0-670-03583-1

This story, about a little girl who has many fears, is set in Pakistan. Saba is afraid of the chickens that chase her and try to bite her toes. She fearfully crosses the courtyard to the bathhouse where she thinks she is safe until she notices a coil near the door. Saba gathers her courage and attempts to kill what she thinks is a snake. She laughs at her fears when she discovers that the coil is merely a tie that holds up one's pants. With relief, Saba gets her revenge and chases the chickens to become Ruler of the Courtyard. (K–3)

 Efforts and courage are not enough without purpose and direction.
—John F. Kennedy

Munch, Robert. *Stephanie's Ponytail.* Annick Press, 1996. ISBN 1-55037-485-0

Each day, Stephanie goes to school wearing her ponytail in a new way. The children laugh and make fun of her. She stands up to them, and they respond by wearing their hair the same way to mock her. Finally Stephanie says she is coming to school with her hair shaved the very next day. The result is humorous and surprising. (1–3)

Primary (grades 1–3)

Couric, Katie. *The Brand New Kid.* Doubleday, 2000. ISBN 0-385-50030-0

Lazlo S. Gasky is the new kid in school and town, and he does not fit in with the rest of the children. They taunt and tease him, and he keeps his head down until Ellie decides to see if she can change how the kids are treating Lazlo. She asks if he would like to play. She spends the afternoon at his house. Lazlo is different because he has an accent, but Ellie knows that if the other kids give him a chance, they will like him. (K–2)

Hopkinson, Deborah. *Sweet Clara and the Freedom Quilt.* Alfred A. Knopf, 1993. ISBN 0-679-82311-5

Sweet Clara, a slave, is taken away from her mother and sent from North Farm to Home Plantation. Aunt Rachel begins to take care of her and teaches Clara how to sew so that she can leave the fields and work in the Big House. In the Big House, Clara hears about the Underground

Railroad and the way north across the Ohio River and beyond to Canada. What the slaves lack is a map, so Clara begins to create one on the quilt she sews. When she finishes the quilt, Sweet Clara leaves it behind for others to study and makes her way north to freedom. (K–3)

 The essence of courage is not that your heart should not quake but that nobody else knows that it does.
—E. B. Benson

Julian, Alison. *Brave as a Bunny Can Be.* Waldman House Press, 2001. ISBN 0-931674-46-8
  Cooper wants to be brave more than anything. One day, after he hears his brothers and sisters talking about him, Cooper goes off to learn how to be brave. He lives by himself, sleeps alone, and takes a trip to the Dark Green Place. At the same time, his brother and sisters look for Cooper. They meet up again when Cooper rescues his sister from the fox and learns a valuable lesson. "Being scared is part of being brave. The brave part is doing your best, even when you're scared." (2–up)

Martin, Bill. *Knots on a Counting Rope.* Henry Holt, 1987. ISBN 0-8050-0571-4
  A grandfather shares with his grandson three of his favorite stories about the day the boy was born, the birth of his horse, and a race. Through it all, the boy overcomes his greatest challenge —blindness—with courage. (K–4)

McCully, Emily Arnold. *Beautiful Warrior: The Legend of the Nun's Kung Fu.* Scholastic, 1998. ISBN 0-590-37487-7
  Kung fu is a means "to physical and mental health and well-being through the development of a vital energy called *qi.* This is a story, which reads like a legend, of Jingyong, who is educated as if she were a son and learns martial arts and kung fu. Jingyong becomes a Buddhist nun and teaches another young girl, Mingyi, kung fu. In one year, Mingyi becomes disciplined and develops the inner strength to win her personal freedom by overpowering the brute, Soong Ling, who threatens her family. (K–5)

Say, Allen. *Tea with Milk.* Houghton Mifflin, 1999. ISBN 0-395-90495-1
  May grows up in the United States, but when she is ready to enter college, her parents move back to Japan and school her in the ways of a Japanese young lady. May rebels against her parents' traditional Japanese ways by moving alone to a large city. She dares to merge the two cultures, meets a young man, marries, and has their first child, the author and illustrator of the book. (2–6)

Stroud, Bettye. *The Patchwork Path: A Quilt Map to Freedom.* Candlewick Press, 2005. ISBN 0-7636-2423-3
  When young Hannah, a Georgia slave, is ten years old, her mother teaches her how to make a quilt. This is going to be a special quilt with a built-in code to help Hannah run to freedom via the Underground Railroad. (0–3)

Winter, Jeannette. *Follow the Drinking Gourd.* Alfred A. Knopf, 1992. ISBN 0-394-89694-7
  Colorful pictures in true American folktale tradition tell the story of a song that helps guide slaves escaping along the Ohio River to the Underground Railroad. (ps–2)

Yin. *Coolies.* Philomel Books, 2001. ISBN 0-399-23227-3
  In the mid-1800s, Shek and his little brother, Wong, leave China for the new land, America. The Chinese laborers are hired to build railroad tracks east to meet up with the Irish laborers who are building tracks west. They call the Chinese "Coolies," lowly workers. Four years later, after

many hardships, East meets West and the two brothers take their savings and ride to San Francisco with the prospect of bringing their family from China. (1–4)

Intermediate (grades 3–5)

Ackerman, Karen. *The Night Crossing.* Alfred A. Knopf, 1994. ISBN 0-679-83169-X
    Clara's family is no longer safe in Austria, and they plan to cross the Swiss border. Clara is determined to take Gittel and Lotte, her two dolls that belong to her grandmother. Many years before when her grandmother was a little girl, she had left Russia with the dolls and crossed the Carpathian Mountains to escape the Cossacks, who burned Jewish homes and businesses. Now Clara thinks to hide the old silver candlesticks inside the dolls as they prepare to leave Austria. At the border, a Nazi soldier tries to frighten Clara into saying something to give her family away, but she remains true to her story and he lets them pass. (3–4)

Bruchac, Joseph. *Skeleton Man.* HarperCollins, 2001. ISBN 0-06-029075-7
    Molly's parents vanish one night. The local authorities are pleased when an elderly man shows up to claim her, stating that he is her great uncle and sharing family photos to prove it. Molly knows this man is not her great uncle, but she does not know how to prove it. He locks her in her room, allowing her to leave only to attend school each day. Molly remembers her dreams about her Mohawk heritage and the Mohawk stories she has heard. She works diligently and solves the mystery of her parents' disappearance. (4–7)

Coerr, Eleanor. *Sadako.* Puffin Books, 1993. ISBN 0-698-11802-2
    Sadako is a picture book for older students about a young girl who is dying of leukemia, which she has as a result of the Hiroshima bombing. This shortened version is enhanced with pastel drawings by Ed Young. (2–6, for older readers)

Curtis, Christopher Paul. *Bud, Not Buddy.* Delacorte Press, 1999. ISBN 0-385-32306-9
    During the Depression, a ten-year-old orphaned runaway boy tries to find his father. He has a few mementos of his Momma in an old suitcase. This is the story of all Bud's adventures on the road to finding his father. (4–7)

Dalgliesh, Alice. *The Courage of Sarah Noble.* Atheneum Books for Young Readers, 1987. ISBN 0-684-18830-9
    Sarah, eight years old, accompanies her father to the wilderness in Connecticut where he builds a house. Mama will stay behind with the younger children, and Sarah will help and cook for her father. Sarah makes friends with the nearby Native Americans. Sarah stays with Tall John and his family while her father fetches her mother and siblings. (1–4)

 A leader must have the courage to act against an expert's advice.
—James Callaghan

Danziger, Paula. *The Cat Ate My Gymsuit.* Delacorte Press, 1974. ISBN 0-385-28183-8
    Marcy Lewis is bored by school, resents her tyrannical father, despairs of ever being thin, and is certain that she'll never have a date. Her new English teacher, Ms. Finney, is a remarkable teacher with unconventional ways, and things begin to change. (4–7)

Edmonds, Walter D. *The Matchlock Gun.* Penguin Putnam, 1989. ISBN 0-399-21911-0
    This classic story won the Newberry Award Medal. It is the story of a Spanish matchlock gun that hung over the fireplace in a settler's home, just outside of Albany, New York, in 1757.

Father shows ten-year-old Edward how to use the heavy old-fashioned gun when he joins the militia to protect Albany. That meant his family was unprotected from the marauding Indians except for the matchlock gun. (3–7) Classic

Lunn, Janet. *Laura Secord: A Story of Courage.* Tundra Books, 2001. ISBN 0-88776-538-6
    Laura Secord is a shy, gentle, Canadian hero who walks twenty miles to warn the British troops of an American plan to overwhelm them during the War of 1812. (3–6)

Myers, Walter Dean. *Patrol: An American Soldier in Vietnam.* HarperCollins, 2002. ISBN 0-06-028364-5
    A young soldier is in the forests of Vietnam when he comes in contact with the enemy. They stare at each other across the field, each unwilling to raise his rifle. A helicopter breaks up the moment, and the young soldier is taken out of harm's way. He lands safely to live another day. (4–up, for older readers)

O'Dell, Scott. *Island of the Blue Dolphins.* Scholastic, 1987. ISBN 0-590-02366-7
    The 1961 Newbery Award winner is the story of a twelve-year-old American Indian girl, Karana, who, during the evacuation of an island off the coast of California, decides to stay with her young brother who is abandoned on the island. After a short time, her brother dies, and Karana is left all alone on the island until she is finally rescued eighteen years later. (4–8)

Pfeffer, Susan Beth. *Beth Makes a Friend.* Delacorte Press, 1998. ISBN 0-385-32583-5
    This book is based on the characters in the book *Little Women* by Louisa May Alcott. Ten-year-old Beth is shy and afraid of her wealthy Aunt March. One afternoon while she is picking apples at her aunt's house, Beth meets poor and ragged Sean O'Neill. Sean is up in a tree stealing apples when he runs away with Aunt March's basket. Sean knows it is wrong to steal, but his hunger overpowers his sense of right and wrong. Beth is very caring and tries to help the O'Neill family by stealing a small silver bowl from her Aunt's house. Her aunt comes upon poor Beth, with surprising consequences. (3–6)

Rodda, Emily. *Rowan of Rin.* Greenwillow Books, 2001. ISBN 0-06-029708-5
    Rowan will never be the man his father was—or will he? Rowan takes care of the bukshah, the gentle animals that graze near the water that flows from the nearby mountain. One day the water stops flowing. The people of Rin decide someone must go up the mountain to find out what is stopping the water from flowing. Several men and women volunteer, and they decide to consult with Sheba who some consider either a witch or a wisewoman. Sheba warns them that the mountain has ways of taming and destroying the bravest among them, and she leaves them with a riddle and a strange map that is only visible when Rowan holds it, thus ensuring his participation in the journey up the mountain. Sheba's words ring in their ears: "Seven hearts the journey make. Seven ways the hearts will break." Rowan, the youngest and most afraid, proves to be brave, wise, and strong. (4–6)

Sperry, Armstrong. *Call It Courage.* Simon & Schuster, 1983. ISBN 0-02-786030-2
    Mafatu's name means Stout Heart, but when his mother drowns, he is very frightened of the sea. His people live near and on the water, so being terrified of it is not an option. When he is twelve years old, he becomes very courageous and overcomes his fear of the sea. (3–6) Classic

Uchida, Yoshiko. *The Bracelet.* Philomel, 1993. ISBN 0-399-22503-X
    It is 1942 in California, during the Japanese internment, and seven-year-old Emi and her Japanese American family are forced to leave their home and friends. Emi receives a parting gift from her friend, a beautiful gold bracelet. She is devastated when she loses the bracelet but soon realizes that she doesn't really need anything to help her to remember her friend. (2–5)

Wells, Rosemary. *Wingwalker*. Hyperion Books for Children, 2002. ISBN 0-7868-0397-5

In this short fiction book, Ruben wins a chance to ride in the passenger seat of a two-seat plane. Ruben vows he will not go higher than his attic window, if only God would keep him away from airplanes. The rest of the story tells how Ruben's family is forced to leave Ambler, Oklahoma, during the Depression and how it came to be that Ruben stands on the wing of the *Land of Cotton* and is, for one moment, a wingwalker. (3–6)

Middle School (grades 5–8)

Ayres, Katherine. *North by Night: A Story of the Underground Railroad*. Yearling Books, 2000. ISBN 0-440-22747-X

The journal of sixteen-year-old Lucinda Spence tells about three months in 1851 when her father decides to turn the Ohio farm into a station on the Underground Railroad. Lucy goes to stay with a sickly neighbor who hides a group of slaves, one of whom is pregnant. Lucy takes the baby to Canada, after the mother dies in childbirth, to ensure its freedom. (5–up)

Berry, James. *Ajeemah and His Son*. Willa Perlman Books, 1991. ISBN 0-06-021043-5

Ajeeman and his son, Atu, are on their way to give a bride gift to the father of Atu's intended. They are captured and taken to the African coast where they are taken aboard a ship and chained to the deck. There is one glimmer of hope: Ajeemah still has the bride gift of gold hidden in his sandals. Both Ajeeman and Atu are taken to Jamaica and sold to separate plantation owners, never to see each other alive again. (6–up)

Billingsley, Franny. *The Folk Keeper*. Atheneum Children's Books, 1999. ISBN 0-689-82876-4

Written in journal format, this is the story of Corinna Stonewall, an orphan from a foundling home, who dresses like a boy in order to work as a folk keeper. She is called by Lord Merton to come to his seaside estate, Cliffsend, in the Northern Isles to be the folk keeper. She discovers that Lord Merton is her father and eventually finds out who her mother is. She takes the job and prides herself on her skills of feeding, distracting, and pacifying the furious, ravenous folk at Cliffsend. She meets someone and falls in love, but in the end she must decide where she really belongs. (5–8)

 Freedom is a system based on courage.
—Charles Peguy

Carbone, Elisa. *Stealing Freedom*. Bantam Doubleday Dell Books for Young Readers, 2001. ISBN 0-440-41707-4,

This story is based on the life of an actual slave, Ann Marie Weems, who has three brothers and one sister. Her father is free, and her mother is a slave. Ann Marie's family is torn from her when her brothers are sold and her mother and sister buy their freedom, leaving Ann Marie behind. Ann Marie disguises herself as a boy and escapes to Canada via the Underground Railroad. (6–10)

Farmer, Nancy. *A Girl Named Disaster*. Scholastic, 1996. ISBN 0-531-09539-8

Ambuya or "Grandmother" is the only one who is kind to Nhamo. A leopard has killed Nhamo's mother, and her father is a murderer. Nhamo is left to be raised by her mother's family. This traditionally is not the custom, and the family expects Nhamo to do all the manual labor. According to Muvuki, the angry spirit of the man Nhamo's father murdered demands that she marry a diseased man with several wives. Ambuya shares a plan with Nhamo and tells her to take what she needs to survive and leave the village. Nhamo takes the family's only canoe and travels from Mozambique to Zimbabwe, where her father's family lives. Her journey is full of perils and dangers, but mystical spirits help her along the way. (6–9)

Goodman, Joan Elizabeth. *Hope's Crossing.* Houghton Mifflin, 1998. ISBN 0-395-86195-0

A party of Tories raids Fairfield, Connecticut, kidnaps young Hope Wakeman, and burns and plunders her home. Hope is taken to Long Island and escapes to New York City with her kidnappers' mother after it is apparent that she is to be sold into slavery. Mother Thomas dies as a result of the pox. Hope turns to a fierce Tory, Pruitt Jones, to help her return to Fairfield and her patriot family. (5–8)

Haddix, Margaret Peterson. *Among the Hidden.* Simon & Schuster, 1998. ISBN 0-689-81700-2

Watch out for the Population Police! This society passes the Population Law after terrible droughts and rationing in an overpopulated world. "They wanted to make sure there would never be more people than the farmer could feed." Therefore, only two children are allowed per family. A third child is a shadow child, hidden and sometimes mistreated, starved, abused, even murdered. Luke spends most of his days in the attic of his house avoiding all windows, peering out of a covered vent. One day he sees a face, a shadow child, Jen, at a neighboring house. Luke breaks all rules and dares to secretly visit Jen, who has access to a computer and is planning a rally of "thirds" to come out of hiding and show themselves to the world at the president's house. Will Jen change the course of history and free the hidden? What part, if any, will Luke play? (4–7)

Lester, Julius. *Pharaoh's Daughter: A Novel of Ancient Egypt.* Silver Whistle, 2000. ISBN 0-15-201826-3

Born into slavery, adopted as an infant by a princess, and raised in the palace of the mighty Pharaoh, Moses tries to figure out who he is. He is loved by three women: his mother, who must give him up, according to the Pharaoh's decree; the Egyptian princess who raises Moses as her own child; and his sister, Almah, who follows the Egyptian deities rather than her Hebrew heritage. The story is told by Moses and his sister Almah. (5–9)

Lisle, Janet Taylor. *The Art of Keeping Cool.* Aladdin Paperbacks, 2000. ISBN 0-689-83788-7

Robert, his sister Caroline, and their mother move from their hog farm in Ohio to Rhode Island. Because they are no longer able to take care of the farm when their father leaves to be a bomber pilot in Europe during World War II, the family moves to be near his estranged parents. As more news about the war reaches the United States, life in the coastal town changes. Large guns are brought to fortify the coast. A local German artist comes under suspicion. Robert's family is secretive about his father. Why did his father leave Rhode Island years before and never come back to his home? Why is his grandfather so controlling, angry, and gruff? Robert will learn that the enemy doesn't have to live across the ocean; the enemy can be in your own home where you are the most vulnerable. (5–7)

Mah, Adeline Yen. *Chinese Cinderella and the Secret Dragon Society.* HarperCollins, 2005. ISBN 0-06-056734-1

Just like Cinderella in the well-known fairy tale, CC is despised by her stepmother because she is too independent. Her stepmother orders her to leave the house, expecting CC to grovel and beg to come back. Instead CC meets Grandmother Wiu and learns the art of martial self-defense. Grandmother Wiu and the four orphans she takes in become involved in the rescue of Americans who bomb the Japanese. CC is proud of her involvement in and the sacrifices she makes for liberation of China against Japanese oppression. (5–8)

Paulson, Gary. *Hatchet.* MacMillan, 1986. ISBN 0-02-527403-1

Thirteen-year-old Brian Robeson is flying to Canada to visit his father when the single-engine plane on which he is a passenger crashes. He is alone in the wilderness, with just a hatchet that was a gift from his mother. He is upset about his parents' divorce, but he must put all of those feelings aside and struggle to survive. (5–9)

Read for Your Life: Tales of Survival from the Editors of Read *Magazine.* Millbrook Press, 1998. ISBN 0-7613-0362-6

"*Read* is a literature magazine published for students in middle and senior high school." This book includes ten stories of survival and courage that first appeared in *Read* magazine. The stories are divided into three sections: ordinary heroes, bad luck or bad judgment, and survival of the fittest. (5–up)

Real courage is when you know you're licked before you begin but you begin anyway and see it through no matter what.
—Harper Lee

Salisbury, Graham. *Jungle Dogs.* Laurel-Leaf Books, 1999. ISBN 0-440-41573-X

"Boy" Regis finds it difficult to stand up for himself because his older brother always gets involved in his problems and teases him for being weak. Boy must find a way to prove his courage by facing the pack of wild dogs that threatens his paper route. (5–8)

YA (grades 8–12)

Albom, Mitch. *The Five People You Meet in Heaven.* Hyperion Press, 2003. ISBN 0-7868-6871-6

Eddie, an eighty-four-year-old repairman at an amusement park, dies in an accident. He meets five people in heaven and learns the part each person played in his life and how he affected them. (General Adult)

Farmer, Nancy. *The Ear, the Eye, and the Arm.* Scholastic, 1994. ISBN 0-531-06829-3

This story takes place in Zimbabwe in the year 2194. Siblings—Tendai, Rita, and Kuda, children of General Amadeus Matsika, the country's chief of security—embark on an adventure. The three overprotected siblings start out by themselves and are kidnapped by the she-elephant who rules the once-toxic waste dump where they mine plastic. The mother and father hire a detective agency, known as "The Ear, the Eye, and the Arm," that is always one-step behind the children. This is a long and unusual story. (7–12)

Frank, Pat. *Alas, Babylon.* Harper Trade, 1999. ISBN 0-06-093139-6

This book is a classic post–nuclear war novel detailing the struggle for survival in a small Florida town. (General Adult)

Lasky, Kathryn. *True North.* Scholastic, 1996. ISBN 0-590-20523-4

Two girls—one white and privileged, one black and a slave—travel together and arrive safely in Canada after several difficult and dangerous months on the Underground Railroad. (7–up)

Lubar, David. *Dunk.* Clarion Books, 2002. ISBN 0-618-19455-X

Chad lives near the Jersey Shore and has always been fascinated by the dunking tank at the amusement park every summer. He wants to get a job as the Bozo who taunts people until he gets dunked in the tank. Chad's father runs out on his family, and therefore many assume that Chad will be a loser, too. (7–10)

Paulson, Gary. *Nightjohn.* Doubleday, 1993. ISBN 0-385-30838-8

A man named Nightjohn risks being beaten and tortured for teaching slaves how to read and write. He sneaks into slave camps at night to give lessons to other slaves. This story tells why the ability to read and write is so important for survival and independence. (6–12)

Spinelli, Jerry. *Stargirl*. Alfred A. Knopf, 2000. ISBN 0-679-88637-0

Stargirl Caraway, a new tenth grader at an Arizona high school, was previously homeschooled. She brings a whole new character to the school—dancing, laughing, wearing long dresses, playing the ukulele, and just being a total nonconformist. At first the students are enchanted, but soon they scorn her. Leo, however, falls in love with her (and is named Starboy by his teasing classmates) and asks her to act normal—with upsetting results. (6–10)

Wynne-Jones, Tim. *The Maestro*. Orchard, 1996. ISBN 0-531-08894-4

Burl Crow lives with his dysfunctional parents—his mother spaces out on drugs, and his father beats him. He escapes into the wilderness and finds a cabin and a pianist who is getting away from his busy life to compose music. Burl stays with him and begins a segment of his life that changes his future. (6–9)

Nonfiction

Adler, David A. *A Picture Book of Sacagawea*. Holiday House, 2000. ISBN 0-8234-1485-X

Sacagawea, or Bird Woman, was captured by the Hidatsa tribe and later sold to Charbonneau, a white trader and trapper. She became his second wife. When Charbonneau was hired to be an interpreter for Lewis and Clark, pregnant Sacagawea accompanied them. Two months later, her son was born and became the youngest member of the expedition. She spent seventeen months with Lewis and Clark; other tribes knew that the group's intentions were friendly because a woman and a baby would not travel with a war party. (2–5)

Bial, Raymond. *The Underground Railroad*. Houghton Mifflin, 1995. ISBN 0-395-69937-1

The author visits the places along the Underground Railroad and recreates the drama and experiences of the runaway slaves and the conductors in this photographic essay. (4–8)

Delano, Marfe Ferguson. *Inventing the Future: A Photo Biography of Thomas Alva Edison*. National Geographic, 2002. ISBN 0-79-226721-4

Many children in the late 1800s did not have formal education. Thomas spent about one or two years in school. His mother homeschooled him, and he developed a love of reading under her direction. When he was twenty-two years old, he invented an electric vote recorder, but no one was interested in purchasing it. This was the first of many patents and inventions. "Negative results are just what I want. They're just as valuable to me as positive results. I can never find the thing that does the job best until I find the ones that don't." (Juvenile)

Fradin, Dennis Brindell. *Bound for the North Star: True Stories of Fugitive Slaves*. Clarion Books, 2000. ISBN 0-395-97017-2

In 1776, there were five hundred thousand slaves in the thirteen colonies. Fifty thousand slaves escaped the South and fled to the North or to Canada. These stories tell about the desperate measures the slaves endured in their quests for freedom. The book notes that slavery still exists today: the "United Nations estimates that 100 million children around the world live in bondage." (5–up)

Freedman, Russell. *Eleanor Roosevelt: A Life of Discovery*. Clarion Books, 1993. ISBN 0-89919-962-7

This photobiography of Eleanor Roosevelt is in the familiar Russell Freedman format. Eleanor was not a pretty child, and she was painfully shy. She married her cousin, Franklin Delano Roosevelt. Eleanor never wanted her husband to become president of the United States. However, from the time she was the first lady until the 1960s, she "was the most famous and at times the most influential woman in the world." (5–8)

Goodman, Susan. E. *Cora Frear: A True Story* (Brave Kids series). Aladdin, 2002. ISBN 0-689-84330-5

> The Brave Kids series features true stories from America's past. This is the story of Cora Frear, who grew up on the prairie at the end of the nineteenth century. She accompanied her father, a doctor, across the prairie to check on a baby with a high fever. On their way across the prairie, they noticed the animals acting strangely and realized that the prairie was on fire. Cora and her father worked together to save themselves and their horses and then continued on to do what they had set out to do. (3–6)

Hearne, Betsy. *Seven Brave Women.* Greenwillow Books, 1997. ISBN 0-688-14502-7

> These are the stories of seven generations of brave women, beginning with a great-great-great-grandmother who lived during the Revolutionary War and ending with a young girl who has a rich history. None of these women fought in any wars, but they showed courage in their everyday lives. (ps–3)

 Keep your fears to yourself but share your courage with others.
—Robert Louis Stevenson

Jiang, Ji-Li. *Red Scarf Girl: A Memoir of the Cultural Revolution.* HarperCollins, 1997. ISBN 0-06-446208-0

> Ji-li was twelve years old when Chairman Mao started the Cultural Revolution. It is 1966 and time to end the evil influences of old ideas, old culture, old customs, and old habits. Ji-li doesn't understand why her mom and dad do not share her enthusiasm for the new campaign. What will the future bring to Ji-li and her family? (5–9)

Littlechild, George. *This Land Is My Land.* Children's Book Press, 1993. ISBN 0-89239-119-7

> George Littlechild honors the wisdom and courage of his Native American ancestors. The illustrations and stories about his people document their suffering at the hands of white men. (3–6)

Philip, Neil. *War and the Pity of War.* Houghton Mifflin, 1998. ISBN 0-395-84982-9

> This book features poetry about all aspects of war from ancient Greece to the twentieth century. The soldier's experiences are similar no matter the time period. The horrors of war, as well the bravery and courage of both the soldiers and civilians, are depicted. (5–up)

Porter, A. P. *Jump at de Sun: The Story of Zora Neale Hurston.* Carolrhoda Books, 1992. ISBN 0-87614-667-1

> Zora Neale Hurston was born in 1891 in Eatonville, Florida, near Orlando. She was the last of five children, and her father never let her forget his disappointment that she was a girl. Zora's mother, Lucy, taught all of her children to jump for the sun—they might not make it, but at least they would get off the ground. Lucy died when Zora was thirteen years old. Zora encountered prejudice for the first time when she had to leave Eatonville and go to Jacksonville. She spent many years wandering, attending school, living in Harlem, and writing and collecting African American tales. Zora wrote four novels, two books of folklore, and an autobiography, as well as articles, essays, short stories, and plays. (4–6)

Provensen, Alice and Martin. *The Glorious Flight: Across the Channel with Louis Bleriot.* Viking, 1983. ISBN 0-670-34259-9

> After many unsuccessful attempts to fly, Louis Bleriot flies across the English Channel in thirty-six minutes on July 25, 1909, in his plane, the *Bleriot XI.* (5–8)

Ryan, Pam Muñoz. *Amelia and Eleanor Go for a Ride*. Scholastic, 1999. ISBN 0-590-96075-X
Eleanor Roosevelt and Amelia Earhart were both independent and daring women. When Amelia comes to the White House and describes what it is like to fly an airplane at night, they decide to fly over Washington, D.C., to see the lights of the city. This historical event took place on April 20, 1933. (1–4)

Sawyer, Kem Knapp. *Anne Frank: A Photographic Story of a Life*. Dorling Kindersley, 2004. ISBN 0-7566-0490-7
Numerous photographs along with historical details and conditions during the war illustrate Anne Frank's short life. The book includes an illustrated timeline and Web sites. (5–10)

St. George, Judith. *Sacagawea*. G. P. Putnam's Sons, 1997. ISBN 0-399-23161-7
Sacagawea is the second wife of a French-Canadian trapper who is an interpreter for Lewis and Clark. Thomas Jefferson appoints Merriwether Lewis to find a water route to the west coast and to establish a presence in the West. All of the information about Sacagawea comes from the journals of Lewis and Clark. There are more memorials to her than any other American woman. (4–6)

 A nation which has forgotten the quality of courage which in the past has been brought to public life is not as likely to insist upon or regard that quality in its chosen leaders today—and in fact we have forgotten.
—John F. Kennedy

Sis, Peter. *Starry Messenger*. Farrar, Straus & Giroux, 1996. ISBN 0-374-37191-1
After learning how a telescope was made, Galileo Galilei made one for himself. He wrote his observations with the telescope in a book titled *The Starry Messenger*. His work became popular, and the Church worried about his theory that the earth was not the center of the universe, which went against biblical teachings. Galileo was tried for heresy. As punishment, he was confined to his house for the rest of his life. The fact that he was imprisoned did not stop Galileo from continuing his work and passing along his ideas. (1–6)

Warren, Andrea. *Escape from Saigon: How a Vietnam War Orphan Became an American Boy*. Farrar, Straus & Giroux, 2004. ISBN 0-374-32224-3
In the span of eight years, Long lost his country and two people he loved. Long is Amerasian. His mother was Vietnamese, and his father was American. His father left Long and his mother when Long was about two years old, and his mother never recovered. When Long was six, his mother took poison and died. Long went to live with his Grandmother Ba, and they moved to Saigon. When Ba could no longer take care of Long, she took him to the Holt Center to be put up for adoption. Conditions in Saigon deteriorated shortly before Long was adopted. He saw his grandmother for the last time and was on one of the few airplanes to make it out of Saigon before it fell to the Communists. Long, or Matthew, adjusted to his new life, family, and school in the United States. (5–9)

Chapter 4

Humor

Related Virtues

Optimism, joy, and enthusiasm

Definition

The quality that makes something laughable or amusing; funniness

Humor in Action

- ✧ Look at the bright side of things.
- ✧ Try to say pleasant things to your classmates to make them smile.
- ✧ Share jokes or funny stories with others.
- ✧ Don't take things too seriously.
- ✧ Be flexible and spontaneous.
- ✧ Laugh at your errors.
- ✧ Support your school—get involved.

People Who Have Demonstrated This Virtue

- ✧ Will Rogers
- ✧ Lucille Ball
- ✧ Bill Cosby
- ✧ Bob Hope
- ✧ Red Skelton
- ✧ Mark Twain

✦ Erma Bombeck

✦ George Burns

✦ Gracie Allen

✦ Goldie Hawn

✦ Shel Silverstein

✦ Lily Tomlin

✦ Joan Rivers

✦ Jerry Seinfeld

✦ Kelsey Grammer

Discussion Questions

✦ Why is it beneficial to have a sense of humor?

✦ Do you know someone who can laugh at himself or herself?

✦ Is laughter contagious?

✦ Do you know someone who consistently makes you laugh?

✦ What is school spirit?

✦ Why is it important to have school spirit?

✦ What makes you laugh?

✦ Do you try to look at the brighter side of things?

✦ Do you enjoy people who are optimistic? Why?

✦ Do your friends have a positive attitude?

✦ Is it important to have a positive attitude?

Related Topics to Explore

✦ Kinds of humor

✦ Fine line between laughing and crying

✦ Muscles used to smile and to frown

✦ Funny bone

✦ Is it healthy to laugh?

✦ Tickling

✦ History of clowns

✦ April Fools' Day

✦ Joker in a deck of cards

✦ Royal jester

✦ Cartoons

✦ Comic books

✦ Comedian teams like Laurel and Hardy

Annotated Titles

Picture Books

Christelow, Eileen. *Where's the Big Bad Wolf?* Clarion Books, 2002. ISBN 0-618-18194-6
    Police Detective Doggedly knows something funny is going on, but he can't quite put his paw on it. He suspects that the Big Bad Wolf is advising the pigs to build houses first out of straw, then sticks, and cardboard. Each time the house is destroyed, the sheep, Esmeralda, comes to the rescue—or is she really a sheep? (1–2)

Fearnley, Jan. *Mr. Wolf's Pancakes.* Little Tiger Press, 1999. ISBN 1-888444-76-2
    Mr. Wolf is very hungry and decides to make pancakes. He asks help from his selfish neighbors, Chicken Little, Wee Willy Winkle, Gingerbread Man, and Little Red Riding Hood. They all refuse until the smell of pancakes drifts out of the kitchen. The story ends with not so surprising results. (ps–3)

Feiffer, Jules. *Bark, George.* HarperCollins, 1999. ISBN 0-06-205930-0
    When George's mother asks him to bark, he meows, quacks, oinks, and moos. George's mother takes him to the vet, and the vet reaches in and pulls out the various animals from inside George. All appears normal until mother asks George to bark once again, and George replies with hello! (ps–2)

Gantos, Jack. *Not So Rotten Ralph.* Houghton Mifflin, 1994. ISBN 0-395-62302-2
    Sarah sends Rotten Ralph to Mr. Fred's Feline Finishing School to learn how to behave, but she is not happy with the results and wishes Rotten Ralph was back to normal. (ps–3)

Gralley, Jean. *Very Boring Alligator.* Henry Holt, 2001. ISBN 0-8050-6328-5
    This story is told in rhyme about a very boring alligator that comes to play and just stays and stays. Even the gator cops play until the little girl yells "stop" and becomes "boss of play every day!" (ps–2)

Marshall, James. *George and Martha Rise and Shine.* Houghton Mifflin, 1976. ISBN 0-395-24738-1
    This book contains five short, humorous stories about two lovable hippos. (0–3)

Mould, Wendy. *Ants in My Pants.* Clarion Books, 2001. ISBN 0-618-09640-X
    Jacob does not want to go to the store with his mum. When she tells him to put on his pants, he says he can't because he has ants in his pants. Jacob continues to find animals in his clothing, which prevents him from getting dressed. When he is finally dressed and surrounded by his imaginary animals, they step outside and realize that it has been snowing. They decide to play in the snow instead of going shopping. Mum says, "Wait just a minute, I will get my hat," but to her surprise, she can't because a cat is in her hat. (ps–2)

Nolen, Jerdine, and Mark Buehner. *Harvey Potter's Balloon Farm.* HarperCollins, 1994. ISBN 0-688-07887-7
    Harvey Potter is a strange man, and this is the story of his U.S. Government–Inspected balloon farm and how he grows them. A young girl watches from a sycamore tree, leaves home, and begins her own balloon farm. (ps–4)

Numeroff, Laura Joffe. *If You Give a Moose a Muffin.* HarperCollins, 1991. ISBN 0-06-024405-4
Give a moose a muffin and see where it leads. (ps–1)

Pilkey, Dav. *Kat Kong.* Harcourt Brace, 1993. ISBN 0-15-242036-3
Mice explorers bring Kat Kong back to Mousopolis to show him off to the other mice. Unfortunately, Kat Kong escapes, and it is Curiosity that kills the cat. (1–3)

Shannon, David. *David Goes to School.* Blue Sky Press, 1999. ISBN 0-590-48087-1
When David is at school, he is always in trouble, constantly hearing, "No, David!" from his teacher. David stays after school until he hears, "Yes, David….You can go home now." (K–3)

Small, David. *George Washington's Cows.* Farrar, Straus & Giroux, 1994. ISBN 0-374-32535-9
This story, told in rhyme, is about George Washington's cows that wear dresses, his pigs that wear wigs, and his sheep that are smarter than he is. George gives up, sells the farm, and decides to try politics. (ps–2)

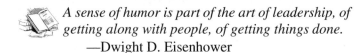

A sense of humor is part of the art of leadership, of getting along with people, of getting things done.
—Dwight D. Eisenhower

Speed, Toby. *Two Cool Cows.* Putnam & Grosset Group, 1995. ISBN 0-399-22647-8
Two cool cows, from the Huckabuck Farm, run away with the new black boots of the Huckabuck kids to jump over the moon and back again all in the same night. (ps–3)

Stanley, Diane. *Saving Sweetness.* G. P. Putnam's Sons, 1996. ISBN 0-399-22645-1
Sweetness runs away from the orphanage only to save the sheriff who is sent to rescue her on more than one occasion. Eventually the sheriff gets it and adopts Sweetness and seven other orphans. (ps–3)

Stevenson, James. *Don't Make Me Laugh.* Farrar, Straus & Giroux, 1999. ISBN 0-374-31827-1
Rules are stated at the beginning of the book: do not laugh or even smile, if you do, then you have to go to the front of the book and start over. The ability to follow the rules is tested in three situations. (ps–1)

Wood, Audrey, and Mark Teague. *Sweet Dream Pie.* Blue Sky Press, 1998. ISBN 0-590-96204-3
For thirteen hours, all the neighbors on Willobee Street think only about the Sweet Dream Pie cooking in Ma's kitchen. Ma warns the neighbors to no avail to eat only one piece. After they devour three or four pieces and promptly fall asleep, the bad dreams and nightmares begin. (ps–2)

Primary (grades 1–3)

Allard, Harry. *The Stupids Take Off.* Houghton Mifflin, 1989. ISBN 0-395-50068-0
Uncle Carbuncle is coming, so the Stupids take an early vacation to avoid him. With their cat at the controls, they take off in their plane and make several stops to visit their other stupid relatives. (K–2)

Cole, Brock. *Buttons.* Farrar, Straus & Giroux, 2000. ISBN 0-374-31001-7
An old man pops the buttons off his pants, and his three daughters all have differing plans on how they will get new buttons for their father. In the process of trying to get new buttons, each of

the girls finds a husband, and only the youngest daughter with the most unlikely plan succeeds in getting the buttons. (1–4)

King-Smith, Dick. *George Speaks.* Millbrook Press, 2002. ISBN 0-7613-1544-6
    Baby George speaks in complete sentences at four weeks of age. George wants to keep it a secret and is amused as his relatives talk baby talk to him. He eventually shares his gift little by little and asks for an encyclopedia for his first birthday. (2–4)

Marcellino, Fred. *I, Crocodile.* Harper Collins, 1999. ISBN 0-06-008859-1
    Rich, imaginative illustrations are an integral part of this story told from the crocodile's point of view. This crocodile was brought back to France by Napoleon, and when the novelty of having a crocodile wears off, he hears talk of crocodile pie. The crocodile escapes to the sewers of Paris, but what about dinner? (ps–3)

Marshall, James. *George and Martha One Fine Day.* Houghton Mifflin, 1978. ISBN 0-395-27154-1
    More adventures with George and Martha in the following chapters, the tightrope, the diary, the icky story, the big scare, and the amusement park. (ps–3)

 Humor and knowledge are two great hopes of our culture.
        —Konrad Lorenz

————. *Rats on the Roof and Other Stories.* Dial Books for Young Readers, 1991. ISBN 0-8037-0834-3
    In these seven silly stories about animals, the author provides humorous characterizations and unpredictable endings. (2-5)

Park, Barbara. *Junie B. Jones Is a Beauty Shop Guy.* Random House Books for Young Readers, 1998. ISBN 0-679-98931-5
    Junie B. Jones accompanies her father to the beauty shop. There Junie discovers a new career and decides she must start practicing cutting hair on her bunny slippers, her dog Tickle, and herself. Junie ends up with sprigs of hair, and with the help of her teacher and father, she returns to the beauty shop for a real haircut. (K–2)

Poploff, Michelle. *Bat Bones and Spider Stew.* Bantam Doubleday Dell, 1998. ISBN 0-385-32557-6
    Henry visits with his new friend Artie Doomsday at his house on top of Hollows Hill. It is Halloween, and jokes are exchanged throughout the dinner. (K–2)

Stanley, Diane. *Rumpelstiltskin's Daughter.* HarperCollins, 1997. ISBN 0-688-14327-X
    This is the story of Rumpelstiltskin's daughter and the same greedy king who makes her mother spin straw into gold. The daughter has a plan, and she outwits the king. He becomes beloved by his subjects and learns there are some things better than gold. (2–4)

Intermediate (grades 3–5)

Anderson, M. T. *Whales on Stilts!* Harcourt, 2005. ISBN 0-15-205340-9
    Twelve-year-old Lily discovers that her father works for a mad scientist who is actually a whale. He is plotting to take over the world by organizing the local whales, who have laser eyes and will soon all be fitted with stilts. Lily's friends, Jasper and Kate, stars of stories of their own (the novels *Horror Hollow* and *Boy Technonaut*) help Lily to save the day and the world. (4–6)

Auch, Mary Jane. *I Was a Third Grade Spy.* Holiday House, 2001. ISBN 0-8234-1576-7
    In this sequel to *I Was a Third Grade Science Project,* Artful, the dog, can talk. In the earlier book, Brian, Josh, and Dougie tried to hypnotize Artful into being a cat, but it was Josh who turned into the cat. In this episode, Artful is sent to spy on the competition in the upcoming talent show. The story is told by Artful and Josh in alternating chapters. (4–6)

Erickson, John R. *The Garbage Monster from Outer Space.* Viking, 1999. ISBN 0-670-88488-X
    Hank, the Cowdog, is head of ranch security. One morning he hears some sounds. Upon investigation, his assistant, Drover, discovers five raccoons tipping over Sally May's garbage cans and scattering the contents. When Hank is caught at the scene, he takes the blame for crimes he didn't commit. (2–5)

McDonald, Megan. *Judy Moody.* Candlewick Press, 2000. ISBN 0-7636-0685-5
    Judy's assignment for school is putting together a "me" collage. Every chapter of the book that follows becomes part of her collage—for example, the funniest thing or the most embarrassing thing that has ever happened to Judy. (3–5)

Pilkey, Dav. *The Adventures of Super Diaper Baby.* Scholastic, 2002. ISBN 0-439-37605-X
    Super Diaper Baby is born and immediately has a disagreement with Deputy Dangerous and his dog. Deputy Dangerous seeks revenge, and his dog rescues Super Diaper Baby and becomes the future Diaper Dog. Together they get rid of Deputy Dangerous, and all live happily ever after. (2–5)

Pinkwater, Daniel. *The Hoboken Chicken Emergency.* Atheneum Children's Books, 1999. ISBN 0-689-83060-2
    Henrietta is a six-foot tall, 266-pound "superchicken" and is loose in the panic-stricken city of Hoboken. (3–6)

_____. *The Lunchroom of Doom.* Atheneum Children's Books, 2000. ISBN 0-689-83846-8
    The werewolf club is banned from the school lunchroom, so they eat at Honest Tom's Tibetan-American Lunchroom and meet many strange customers. (2–5)

Sachar, Louis. *Wayside School Gets a Little Stranger.* HarperCollins, 1995. ISBN 0-688-13694-X
    First, Wayside School was closed for 242 days because of the invasion of the cows. Now the most beloved teacher, Mrs. Jewls, is out for maternity leave, and the students have to endure a few very strange substitutes. (4–7)

Scieszka, Jon. *2095.* Puffin Books, 1995. ISBN 0-670-85795-5
    Another zany adventure of the Time Warp Trio begins with the trio visiting the Museum of Natural History where they are transported into the future, to 2095. Sam, Fred, and Joe are part of the 1990s exhibit until three people contracted by an agency show up. The boys are rescued by Jonie, Samantha, and Frieda, who happen to be their great-grandkids. The girls want to make sure the trio returns to the past so that they—the girls—will have a future. (2–6)

_____. *See You Later, Gladiator.* Viking, 2000. ISBN 0-670-89340-4
    Sam, Fred, and Joe—the Time Warp Trio—are traveling again, this time to ancient Rome where they are in Gladiator School. They participate in a horrendous food fight, battle a huge, hairy gladiator, and play in the sacred Temple of Vesta. (2–5)

_____. *The True Story of the 3 Little Pigs!* Viking Kestrel, 1989. ISBN 0-670-89779-5
    This classic story is told from the wolf's point of view. (1–up)

Middle School (grades 5–8)

Hiaasen, Carl. *Flush.* Random House, 2005. ISBN 0-375-82182-0

    In the Florida Keys, brother and sister Noah and Abbey try to help their father, who is serving time in jail for sinking a gambling boat, the *Coral Queen.* The father claims that the boat is illegally pumping raw sewage into the water rather than using the appropriate on-shore tank. Some unlikely people help them along the way, and the son of the boat's owner bothers them, but in the end, they prove their claim. (5–up)

Klise, Kate. *Regarding the Fountain: A Tale in Letters, of Liars and Leaks.* HarperCollins, 1998. ISBN 0-380-97538-6

    This mystery is told entirely in letters, faxes, memos, and newspaper articles. Dry Creek Middle School has a broken water fountain, and the principal writes to a water fountain company requesting a catalog. He gets a response from Florence Waters, the fountain designer who connects with a fifth-grade class for suggestions. These students are working on a project about the history of the town of Dry Creek, and they discover lots of interesting and incriminating information. In the end, Florence Waters provides the school with a water fountain extraordinaire. It has swimming, fishing, and ice skating and includes a geyser, a whirlpool, and a walrus named Wally! (4–7)

Paterson, Katherine. *Preacher's Boy.* Clarion Books, 1999. ISBN 0-395-83897-5

    Robbie is eleven years old and the son of a preacher. He is full of mischief, especially after he hears a sermon stating that the end of the world may be within six months of the turn of the century. He decides to be an atheist so he won't have to bother with the Ten Commandments. His one ambition is to ride in a motorcar before the world goes bust. Never mind the fact that he has only seen one motorcar in his life. How Robbie achieves his dream is a humorous and entertaining read. (5–up)

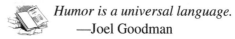

Humor is a universal language.
—Joel Goodman

Paulsen, Gary. *Harris and Me.* Harcourt Brace, 1993. ISBN 0-15-292877-4

    A young boy is placed with some distant relatives on a farm for the summer. It will be the first time that he experiences love and a family. He becomes fast friends with his cousin Harris, and together they get into numerous, hilarious adventures. (4–7)

Sachar, Louis. *Holes.* Farrar, Straus & Giroux, 1998. ISBN 0-374-33265-7

    Stanley Yelnats IV's, great-grandfather lost his entire fortune, and a curse is placed on his descendants. Stanley is sent to Camp Green Lake for a crime he didn't commit. Camp Green Lake is not at all what its name suggests. It is desolate and barren with no water in sight, so fences and guards are unnecessary. Stanley's punishment is to dig a hole five feet by five feet in width and depth every day in the hot sun before he is allowed to do anything else. Everything changes when Stanley finds a small gold tube with the initials of KB. This book won the Newbery Award in 1999 and was made into a movie. (5–8)

Shusterman, Neal. *The Schwa Was Here.* Dutton Children's Books, 2004. ISBN 0-525-47182-0

    Eighth-grader Calvin Schwa is invisible, or at least it seems that he is not seen or noticed by friends, classmates, and family. He makes friends with Antsy, short for Anthony, who has seen several instances in which Calvin was in the middle of things but went totally unnoticed. Calvin has major family issues, and even though Antsy's intentions are good, he actually makes things worse for Calvin. (6–8)

Snicket, Lemony. *The Bad Beginning.* HarperCollins, 1999. ISBN 0-06-051828-6

> This is the first book in the series A Series of Unfortunate Events. The author warns you that this is a book without a happy ending. The three Baudelaire youngsters are wealthy orphans after their parents perish in a fire that destroys their home. The executor of the will sends them to live with Count Olaf, a distant relative who treats them cruelly. Count Olaf is an actor, who schemes to take their money by including the children in a play and marrying the oldest girl, Violet. If the children do not comply, Count Olaf threatens to kill the baby. Clever Violet saves the situation, but Count Olaf escapes to plan more treachery. (4–7)

Tolan, Stephanie. *Surviving the Applewhites.* HarperCollins, 2002. ISBN 0-06-623602-9

> Jake Semple is a juvenile delinquent who has recently been expelled from another school. He ends up at the Applewhite's home school, Creative Academy, on their farm called Wit's End. Each of the Applewhites is a unique individual, and the only normal one is their daughter E. D., who tries to set up a curriculum and keep the homeschooling organized. Jake first resists their attempts to include him but eventually gets drawn into Mr. Applewhite's little theater presentation of *The Sound of Music,* which is staged in the barn. (5–up)

YA (grades 8–12)

Anderson, M. T. *Burger Wuss.* Turtleback Books, 2001. ISBN 0-6062-2539-0

> When Anthony's girlfriend leaves him for someone else, Anthony is devastated. Her new boyfriend is an exemplary employee at a burger restaurant, so Anthony gets a job at a rival burger place. He then creates an elaborate plan for revenge. (8–10)

Elish, Dan. *Born Too Short: The Confessions of an Eighth-Grade Basket Case.* Atheneum, 2002. ISBN 0-6898-4386-0

> Matt is very jealous of his best friend Keith, who has everything. One day, when Matt has had enough, he wishes that things will begin to go wrong for Keith. Matt finds his first girlfriend just as things really do start going badly for Keith, and Matt is consumed with guilt. (7–9, for mature readers)

 Humor is laughing at what you haven't got when you ought to have it.
—Langston Hughes

Korman, Gordon. *Son of the Mob.* Hyperion Press, 2002. ISBN 0-7868-0769-5

> Seventeen-year-old Tony Luca's family is in the "vending machine business," and his father is King of the Mob. Tony disassociates himself with it all, but still the family interferes with his life. He gets thrown in jail when it is discovered that the Porsche he got for his sixteenth birthday is "hot." He meets Kendra and falls in love but soon discovers that her father is an FBI agent—in fact, he is the FBI agent who is bugging and wiretapping the family house. In the end, Tony is successful at being part of his family by preserving his self-respect, keeping his conscience clear, and maintaining his relationship with Kendra. (7-up)

Tashjian, Janet. *The Gospel According to Larry.* Henry Holt, 2001. ISBN 0-8050-6378-1

> Josh, a loner, starts a Web site hoping to change the world. The sometimes-witty site is devoted to anticonsumerism. As the Web site receives more and more attention, one person is determined to find out who "Larry" (a.k.a. Josh) is. When she arrives at his house with cameraman in tow, life changes for Josh for good. His message is lost in the media frenzy, and he experiences celebrity worship firsthand. (7-up)

Van Draanen, Wendelin. *Flipped.* Alfred A. Knopf, 2001. ISBN 0-375-81174-5

Told from the viewpoints of Bryce and Juli, this tale begins in second grade when Bryce moves into the neighborhood and Juli anxiously awaits his arrival. Bryce's father immediately thinks she is a pest, and Bryce agrees. Bryce does everything to avoid Juli. Fast forward to eighth grade. Juli is not afraid to speak her mind and sits in a beloved sycamore tree when the owner tries to cut it down. After Juli appears in the newspaper supporting her cause, Bryce's grandfather becomes interested in her because Juli reminds him of his deceased wife. Bryce begins to look at Juli in a new way; at the same time, Juli sees through the shallowness of Bryce. (5–9)

Nonfiction

Collins, David R. *Mark T-W-A-I-N! A Story about Samuel Clemens.* Carolrhoda Books, 1994. ISBN 0-87614-801-1

When Samuel Clemens grew up in Hannibal, Missouri, he thought it was a "boy's paradise." Sammy did not like school; it bored him. When his father died, he quit school, and at twelve years old he went to work for a printer. Samuel Clemens had many childhood experiences that appear in his humorous writings. "I was fortunate to survive my childhood, although there are some folks who might think my survival was unfortunate." (3–6)

 Humor is a spontaneous, wonderful bit of an outburst that just comes. It's unbridled, it's unplanned, it's full of surprises.
—Erma Bombeck

Herbert, Solomon J., and George H. Hill. *Bill Cosby.* Chelsea House, 1999. ISBN 0-7910-1121-6

Bill Cosby grew up in North Philadelphia and is the eldest of four boys. His father was unable to support the family, and eventually he stopped coming around. His mother worked long hours as a domestic, and it was up to Bill to keep his brothers out of trouble. Much of Bill's comic material comes from these difficult growing-up years. Bill was an outstanding athlete and student. He liked to make people laugh. He started as a stand-up comic in his second year at Temple University and began pursuing the most difficult thing he would do—breaking into show business. (4–7)

Keating, Frank. *Will Rogers: An American Legend.* Silver Whistle Harcourt, 2002. ISBN 0-15-202405-0

Humorist Will Rogers, the youngest of eight children, was born in Oklahoma in 1879; he died in 1935. This brief biography is interspersed with his wise and witty sayings, for example, "A man only learns by two things, one is reading, and the other is association with smarter people." The oil-on-canvas illustrations on opposing pages are by Mike Wimmer. (1–4)

Chapter 5

Responsibility

Related Virtues

Gratitude, self-awareness, and self-esteem, self-discipline, accountability, reliability, and trustworthiness

Definition

The state, quality, or fact of being responsible; something for which one is responsible; a duty, obligation, or burden

Responsibility in Action

✧ Complete and turn in your homework and assignments.

✧ Keep your locker or cubby clean.

✧ Clean up after yourself in your classroom and the cafeteria.

✧ Do your share of the work when you are part of a group.

✧ Assist your teacher without being asked.

✧ Participate in beach or park cleanup.

✧ Clean your room without being asked.

✧ Feed and take good care of your pets.

✧ Make appropriate food choices.

✧ Follow through on your promises or obligations.

✧ If you take lessons, make sure you practice.

✧ If you join a team, make sure you play in all the games and go to all the practices.

People Who Have Demonstrated This Virtue

- ✧ Golda Meir
- ✧ Jane Goodall
- ✧ Herbert Hoover
- ✧ Elizabeth Cady Stanton
- ✧ Booker T. Washington
- ✧ Lyndon B. Johnson
- ✧ Alan Greenspan
- ✧ Janet Reno
- ✧ Sandra Day O'Connor
- ✧ Ralph Nader
- ✧ Harry Truman
- ✧ Johnny Appleseed
- ✧ Sammy Sousa

Organizations

- ✧ Greenpeace
- ✧ Humane Society of the United States
- ✧ World Wildlife
- ✧ Sierra Club
- ✧ Amnesty International
- ✧ National Audubon Society
- ✧ National Wildlife Federation
- ✧ National Wildlife Refuge Association
- ✧ Earth Force for Kids
- ✧ United Nations Environment Program

Discussion Questions

- ✧ Are you a dependable member of your family?
- ✧ Can your parents count on you?
- ✧ Is it sometimes difficult to honor your commitments? When?
- ✧ Tell three things that someone might do to demonstrate responsibility for the earth.
- ✧ Why is it important to demonstrate legal responsibility?
- ✧ Are you able to stick to the goals you set for yourself?
- ✧ Do you do your part in group work?

Related Topics to Explore

- ✧ Respect for elderly
- ✧ Examples of respect in other cultures
- ✧ Personal and global—earth-friendly

✧ Rain forest

✧ Extinction

✧ Exercise, health, brain, and body

✧ Responsibility in advertising

✧ Pet ownership and overpopulation

✧ Deforestation

✧ World conservation

Annotated Titles

Picture Books

Alborough, Jez. *Fix-It Duck.* HarperCollins, 2001. ISBN 0-06-000699-4

Duck sits down to have a cup of tea when a drip drops into his cup. "This is a job for fix-it duck." This leads to one mishap after another, and in the end Duck realizes his roof is not leaking but that he forgot to turn off the water in his bathtub! (ps–1)

Cherry, Lynne. *The Shaman's Apprentice: A Tale of the Amazon Rain Forest.* Harcourt Brace, 1998. ISBN 0-15-201281-8

In the Amazon rain forest, young Kamanya, of the Tirio tribe, hopes to become the tribe's next shaman. He tries to learn everything he can from the tribe's current shaman. Missionaries bring new diseases to the tribe, and they also bring pills to cure the diseases. Soon the tribe turns away from its dependence on plants for medicine. Eventually, an ethnobotanist comes to the rain forest and studies the plants, restoring the people's faith in their medicinal values. (1–4)

Pilkey, Dav. *Dog Breath: The Horrible Trouble with Hally Tosis.* Blue Sky Press, 1994. ISBN 0-590-47466-9

Mr. and Mrs. Tosis are going to get rid of their dog, Hally, because she has such terrible breath until two burglars break into their house. Hally gives the two burglars a great big kiss, and they are out cold. After winning a reward for capturing the burglars and showing her responsibility for her home and family, Hally becomes famous, and they decide to keep their unusual watchdog. (ps–3)

 Man must cease attributing his problems to his environment, and learn again to exercise his will— his personal responsibility.
—Albert Schweitzer

Shannon, David. *Duck on a Bike.* Blue Sky Press, 2002. ISBN 0-439-05023-5

One day Duck gets the idea that he can ride a bike. When he does and shows off in front of all the other animals, they, too, would like to ride a bike. They get their chance when a group of kids leave their bikes unattended in front of their house. Now Duck has other ideas. (ps–2)

Primary (grades 1–3)

Battan, Mary. *Hey Daddy! Animal Fathers and Their Babies.* Peachtree, 2002. ISBN 1-56145-272-6

The author describes the role of the daddy in nature—to care for and protect the newborns, including humans. "It takes someone very special to be a good daddy." (1–4)

Cowley, Joseph. *Agapanthus Hum and the Eyeglasses.* Penguin Putnam, 2001. ISBN 0-698-11883-9

Agapanthus is called Hum because she hums like a button on a string when she twirls, twists, and cartwheels. It is her eyeglasses that suffer most. Finally she decides to give her glasses to her good little mother to hold while she does her acrobatics. (00–3)

Diakite, Baba Wague. *The Hunterman and the Crocodile.* Scholastic, 1997. ISBN 0-590-89828-0

The crocodile and his family are on a pilgrimage to Mecca when they run out of food and are exhausted. When the hunterman comes upon them, the crocodile asks if he will take them back to the river. The crocodile promises that he will not harm the hunterman. The hunterman stacks the crocodiles on his head and returns them to the river. The crocodile goes back on his promise and threatens to eat the hunterman. All of the animals refuse to interfere because of the way humans treat animals. Eventually the hunterman is let go, but not before he learns the importance of living in harmony with nature. (ps–2)

Goldman, Lisa, and Linda K. Garvey. *A Day with Dirtbike.* Disney Press, 1988. ISBN 0-7868-4321-7

Doug and Judy's parents help grandma who has sprained her ankle. Judy offers Doug thirty-five dollars if he will take care of Cleopatra Dirtbike. Doug tries his best, but when Judy returns home, she has never seen the house in such a mess. (2–4)

McCully, Emily Arnold. *The Bobbin Girl.* Dial Books for Young Readers, 1996. ISBN 0-8037-1827-6

The story takes place in a textile mill in the 1830s in Lowell, Massachusetts. It is based on a true story. Ten-year-old Rebecca Putney works in the mill as a bobbin girl to help her mother make ends meet. Her mother owns a boarding house for women who work in the mill. The women work long hours, the machinery is noisy, the air in the mill is unhealthy, there is a high injury rate, and the wages are poor. When the mill owners threaten to lower the wages, the women protest by staging a "turn out" (strike), and Rebecca participates. (ps–3)

Pilkey, Dav. *Ricky Ricotta's Giant Robot vs. the Voodoo Vultures from Venus.* Scholastic, 2001. ISBN 0-439-23624-X

This is the third book in the series of Ricky, a small rodent with glasses and his pal, a giant robot with rodent ears. The two are late for dinner so their punishment is that they cannot watch the TV show *Rocky Rodent*. In this case, being punished turns into a good thing. The last part of the book gives instructions on how to create your own flip-o-rama. (ps–3)

Sachar, Louis. *Marvin Redpost: Alone in His Teacher's House.* Random House, 1994. ISBN 0-679-81949-5

Marvin's teacher is going away for the week, and she asks Marvin to take care of her old dog, Waldo. Marvin does his best but is concerned when Waldo stops eating. The vet suggests that he cook some liver to feed to Waldo, because he figures the old dog just misses his owner. When Waldo dies, how will Marvin ever face Mrs. North again? Will she think that Marvin was irresponsible? (0–3)

Teague, Mark. *Pigsty*. Scholastic, 1994. ISBN 0-5904-5915-5

Wendell Fultz never cleans his room, and his mother finally gives up and tells him to live in a pigsty if that is the way he likes it. Soon four pigs move in to share his room. Wendell deals with it for a while but soon runs out of patience when they hog the covers, chew his baseball cards, and get hoof prints on his comic books. (1–4)

Intermediate (grades 3–5)

Avi. *The Secret School*. Harcourt, 2001. ISBN 0-152-1637-57

Ida Bidson attends eighth grade in a one-room school in rural Colorado in 1925. About a month and a half before the end of school, the teacher leaves, and the school board decides to close the school. Ida must take her exams so she can go on to high school to become a teacher, but no one seems to think it is important for a girl to have an education. At her friend's urging, Ida secretly keeps the school open and acts as the teacher as she studies and continues with all her farm chores at home. (3–6)

Byars, Betsy. *Me Tarzan*. HarperCollins, 2000. ISBN 0-602-8706-3

Dorothy gets the role of Tarzan in the class play, and each time she rehearses her yell, she attracts more and more animals from the surrounding areas. (2–5)

Christopher, Matt. *Mountain Bike Mania*. Little, Brown and Company, 1998. ISBN 0-316-14292-1

Will's parents encourage him to find a sport that he enjoys doing after school. Will discovers that he loves mountain biking but at the same time almost loses his best friend. (3–7)

Dorris, Michael. *Guests*. Hyperion Books for Children, 1994. ISBN 0-7868-0047-X

Moss is not pleased that his father has invited white guests to the village's special harvest meal, so he goes off to sulk about it. He meets up with a distant relative, Trouble, and without preparation, he goes off to the forest for his "away time" and returns with a greater understanding. (3–7)

Hurst, Carol Otis. *In Plain Sight*. Houghton Mifflin, 2002. ISBN 0-618-19699-4

When her father leaves for the California Gold Rush, Sarah's mother is forced to work in a factory to hire help to run the farm. Young Sarah stays home from school to take care of the house and her brother and sister. Sarah does not mind because she loves her fun-filled father and doesn't understand her mother's sternness. Gradually she realizes her mother's love in her day-to-day actions. (4–6)

Hurwitz, Johanna. *One Small Dog*. HarperCollins, 2000. ISBN 0-688-17382-9

Curtis is a fourth grader who lives with his mother and younger brother in an apartment. Curtis's mom and dad are getting divorced, and to compensate, his mom gives in to Curtis and allows him to get a dog at the animal shelter. It turns out that the puppy, Sammy, is a chewer and then a biter. He bites the brother, the mother, and finally Curtis, who needs six stitches to close the wound. After just two short weeks, Curtis must give up the dog to a friend of his father's who has the time, patience, and space to train him. Good advice is featured at the end of the book from a dog trainer regarding proper puppy training. This is a good reminder that dog ownership is a big responsibility. (2–5)

Kinsey-Warnock, Natalie. *Lumber Camp Library*. HarperCollins, 2002. ISBN 0-06-029321-7

Ruby, firstborn of eleven children, grows up in a lumber camp. She is close to her father who wants her to become a teacher. When Pa drowns in a logjam, the family moves closer to town, and the lumberjacks hire mother to cook for them. Eventually Ruby teaches them how to read. Ruby meets blind Mrs. Graham who has a houseful of books, and Ruby and her family move in with Mrs. Graham. Ruby fulfills her father's wish that she become a teacher, and she puts together a Lumber Camp Library. (Juvenile)

 People need responsibility. They resist assuming it, but they cannot get along without it.
—John Steinbeck

Skurzynski, Gloria. *Deadly Waters.* National Geographic Society, 1999. ISBN 0-7922-7655-8
Jack, Ashley, and a foster child named Bridger help solve the mystery of why manatees are dying in Florida. During their adventure, they also learn about the Florida Everglades' ecosystem and wildlife. (3–7)

Vander Velde, Vivian. *Wizard at Work.* Harcourt Children's Books, 2003. ISBN 0-1520-4559-7
The wizard has had a busy school year with his students at wizard school. For the summer, he wants to read, do some gardening, relax, go fishing, and just enjoy himself. This doesn't happen; his friends and neighbors feel he has a responsibility to them, and they keep coming to him for help with a spell to rescue a princess, among other things. (3–6)

Middle School (grades 5–8)

Cabot, Meg. *Princess in Love.* HarperCollins, 2002. ISBN 0-06-029467-1
The third in the series, her Royal Highness Princess Amelia Mignonette Grimaldi Thermopolis Renaldo of Genovia, also known as Mia, is preparing for her introduction to the people of Genovia. Mia is also trying to figure out what to do about her present boyfriend. (6–9)

Carter, Alden R. *Bull Catcher.* Scholastic, 1997. ISBN 0-590-50959-4
Neil Larsen, nicknamed Bull, starts to think about baseball in November, even though the season doesn't start until April. His best friend Jeff plays shortstop, and Bull is the catcher. They play together in middle school, and the book is divided into their four years at Shiply High School. The highlight of every year is the game with Caledonia. Three years in a row, they lose the final game of the season. Senior year will be different. It is dedicated to Billy who died in a tragic car crash. Bull wants to win this championship and final game—that would be enough because "it was never quite the same after Billy died." (7–up)

Danziger, Paula, and Ann M. Martin. *P.S. Longer Letter Later.* Scholastic Press, 1998. ISBN 0-590-21310-5
Tara Starr, whose voice is author Paula Danziger, moves away to Ohio with her very young parents who are getting their life together. Elizabeth, whose voice is Ann M. Martin, comes from a well-to-do stable family that falls apart when her father loses his job and eventually leaves. The story is told though the correspondence between the two twelve year olds. (4–7)

Fletcher, Ralph. *Flying Solo.* Bantam Doubleday Dell Books, 2000. ISBN 0-440-41601-9
A group of sixth-grade students decide to run the class for the day when the substitute for their teacher does not appear. Clearly, their teacher, Mr. Fabiano, has made an impression with a strict routine, because they do a good job of running the class and discussing issues affecting both individuals and the class as a whole. (4–8)

Giff, Patricia Reilly. *Nory Ryan's Song.* Random House, 2002. ISBN 0-440-41829-1
Twelve-year-old Nory Ryan, her two older sisters, and their younger brother live with their grandfather. Da, their father, is working in Galway to send money home. Times are hard, and increasingly they worry about food and the dreaded potato blight. Neighbors who cannot pay the

rent are put into the street by their English landlords, and their huts are torn down. Nory develops a relationship with Anna, who at first frightens her but will prove to be Nory's salvation. (5–8)

Hesse, Karen. *Phoenix Rising*. Henry Holt, 1994. ISBN 0-805-03108-1

A catastrophic accident at a Vermont nuclear power plant sends two refugees with severe radiation poisoning to thirteen-year-old Nyle Sumner and her grandmother's sheep farm. Gran and Nyle tend their sheep while they wear protective masks. They also tend to the refugees, Mrs. Trent and her son, Evan. Nyle has a difficult time because not too long ago she had watched both her mother and grandfather die from natural causes. She handles all this responsibility with simple acts of kindness and steady, sensible care of the farm and the refugees. (6–8)

Hiaasen, Carl. *Hoot.* Knopf, 2002. ISBN 0-375-82181-3

On the bus going to his new school, Roy notices a barefoot boy running down the street one day. This is the first thing that has interested Roy since he moved to Florida, so he makes several inquiries. At the same time, a particular piece of property is to become the new Mother Paula's All-American House of Pancakes—that is, if they can stop the vandalism long enough to begin bulldozing the property. Roy learns that the barefoot boy, Mullet Fingers, is the one who is causing the delays, hoping to discourage the property owners in order to save threatened burrowing owls. (5–8)

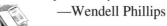

Responsibility educates.
—Wendell Phillips

Holman, Sheri. *Sondok: Princess of the Moon and Stars.* Scholastic, 2002. ISBN 0-439-16586-5

These diary entries are messages placed in the ancestral jar of Sondok's grandmother and describe one year in her life. Sondok will be the first queen regent of any Korean kingdom because her father has no heirs. (4–8)

Lasky, Kathryn. *Marie Antoinette: Princess of Versailles.* Scholastic, 2000. ISBN 0-439-07666-8

Two years in the life of Marie Antoinette, future Queen of France, are described in her diary entries beginning when she is thirteen and politically betrothed to Louis Auguste, dauphin of France. To prepare her for this awesome responsibility, she learns to write, read, speak French (she was born in Vienna, Austria), dress, act, and even breathe according to French Court etiquette. (4–8)

Lowry, Lois. *The Giver.* Houghton Mifflin, 1993. ISBN 0-395-64566-2

Twelve-year-old Jonas lives in a seemingly ideal world. Not until he is given his life assignment as the Receiver does he demonstrate responsibility as he tries to understand the dark secrets behind this fragile community. (7–9)

Lubar, David. *Hidden Talents.* Turtleback Books, 2000. ISBN 0-606-20703-1

After being expelled from a number of schools, thirteen-year-old Martin Anderson is now a student at a publicly funded alternative school. His roommate, Torchie, denies having anything to do with the fires that seem to start where he is. Eventually, Martin realizes that some of his friends have very unusual powers—one is telepathic, one is telekinetic, and one is clairvoyant. He gets them to work together to save the school from one student's attempt to sabotage a state inspection. (6–8)

Philbrick, Rodman. *The Young Man and the Sea.* Blue Sky Press, 2004. ISBN 0-439-36829-4

Skiff hears his mother talking to him, long after she has died. She asks Skiff to look after his father, but Skiff would have done that anyway. His father is not interested in anything except his beer, TV, and the couch. Skiff wants to show everyone that he is not a "swamper," so he sets out in his ten-foot boat with a bucket of bait and some peanut butter and jelly sandwiches. He takes his boat thirty-five miles off shore in search of blue fin tuna and an exciting adventure. (5–8)

Rawls, Wilson. *Where the Red Ferns Grow.* Bantam Books, 1997. ISBN 0-553-25585-1
   Bill and his coonhound dogs have many adventures in the Ozarks. The threesome hunts raccoons and become quite successful. A confrontation with a mountain lion turns deadly, and Billy learns about the old Native American legend of the sacred red ferns that grow over the graves of beloved dogs. (5–10)

 Responsibility is the price of greatness.
   —Winston Churchill

Ryden, Hope. *Wild Horse Summer.* Dell Books, 1997. ISBN 0440-415-489
   Alison doesn't want to leave her Chicago home and friends to spend the summer at a ranch in Wyoming. She will have to celebrate her thirteenth birthday there and is fearful that she will spend the whole summer taking care of her cousin, Kelly, who is blind. She is afraid of heights, so she takes the train to Wyoming. At first she is frightened of riding horses because of their height. As it turns out, Kelly is very independent and helps Alison get over her fear of heights. Soon Alison loves riding horses and even flies back to Chicago. (4–6)

Yep, Laurence. *The Tiger's Apprentice.* HarperCollins, 2003. ISBN 0-0600-1013-4
   Tom, an eighth grader, discovers that he has magical powers inherited from his Chinese grandmother and learns that he is part of a group that must protect a talisman that can bring either peace or destruction to the world. (5–7)

YA (grades 8–12)

Anderson, Laurie Halse. *Catalyst.* Viking, 2002. ISBN 0-670-03566-1
   Kate Malone is a high school senior, an advanced placement chemistry student, and a persistent runner. Calculus and physics are easy. Her father is a minister; her mother died nine years earlier. Kate is driven to the point of exhaustion in her goal of getting into MIT—her mother's alma mater and the only school to which Kate has applied. She takes care of the household single-handedly, even when her father invites Kate's enemy, Teri, and her younger brother to share Kate's room when their house burns down. (8–up)

Chevalier, Tracy. *Girl with a Pearl Earring.* HarperCollins Publishers, 1999. ISBN 0-00-225890-0
   Sixteen-year-old Griet goes to work as a maid in the Vermeer household because her father has gone blind. She has a keen sense of color, and Vermeer makes her his assistant and she poses for his famous painting, *Girl with a Pearl Earring.* (YA)

Cooney, Caroline B. *Code Orange.* Random House, 2005. ISBN 0-385-73259-7
   Mitty Blake barely gets by in school. In his science class, his term paper is to be on an infectious disease. Mitty explores an old medical book and locates an envelope with the words *Scabs-VM epidemic, 1902, Boston.* Mitty taps the contents of the envelope into his hand, it crumbles, and he returns the contents back to the envelope. Mitty than rubs his nose and thinks nothing of what he has done until later. As Mitty learns more about his chosen disease, smallpox, he becomes worried that he may have contracted the disease. He knows that in twelve to fourteen days, he may exhibit the symptoms. Others are interested in Mitty also, but for all the wrong reasons. Terrorists kidnap him because smallpox is at the top of the list of feared methods of bioterrorism. It is up to Mitty to prevent the terrorists from carrying out their plans. (7–up)

_____. *Driver's Ed.* Delacorte Press, 1994. ISBN 0-385-32087-6

Remy and Morgan accept a challenge to steal highway signs. Along with Nickie who is driving, they steal three signs, including a stop sign. Later that night, a young mother dies in a tragic car accident at the same corner where they had stolen the stop sign. The woman's husband appears on television and offers a reward to anyone with information about the vandalism that led to his wife's death. (7–up)

 The game is my life. It demands loyalty and responsibility, and it gives me back fulfillment and peace.
—Michael Jordan

Ferris, Jean. *Of Sound Mind.* Farrar, Straus & Giroux, 2001. ISBN 0-374-35580-0

Theo is a senior in high school, and his parents and brother are overly dependent on him because he is the only member of his family who can hear. Theo's father does not take advantage of Theo, but the situation changes when his father suffers a stroke and his care is left up to Theo. With all of this responsibility, how can Theo think about going to college? (8–up)

Freeman, Anne. *The Cuckoo's Child.* Greenwillow Books, 1996. ISBN 0-688-14290-7

Mia lives with her parents and two stepsisters in Beirut in the 1960s. Her parents take a boat trip to Greece and are lost at sea. Mia goes to live with her aunt in Ionia, Tennessee, while her stepsisters go to visit their real father in Boston. Both Mia and her aunt have a difficult time adjusting to their new responsibilities. (YA)

Giles, Gail. *Shattering Glass.* Roaring Brook Press, 2002. ISBN 0-7613-1581-0

Rob Haynes, a transfer student, quickly becomes the most popular student at his new high school. He has a plan: he and his small circle of friends plan to take on the class nerd. Simon Glass is their project, they want to turn him into the class favorite. They take him clothes shopping, get his hair styled, put him on a diet, and teach him how to drive. Simon becomes more popular each day, eventually challenging Rob's position. The final results are bloody, deadly, and tragic. (9–up)

Griffin, Adele. *Dive.* Hyperion Books for Children, 1999. ISBN 0-7868-1567-1

Ben is eleven years old and chooses to live with his stable stepfather. Half-brother Dustin leaves his father and goes to live with his restless stepmother who is Ben's mother. Ben and the stepfather rush to California to be at Dustin's side when he is hospitalized as a result of a diving accident—or was it an accident? Ben relays the story, confronts his mother, and realizes Dustin's self-destructive tendencies. (7–10)

Lynch, Chris. *Shadow Boxer.* Peter Smith Publishers, 1997. ISBN 0-8446-6886-9

Fourteen-year-old George and his younger brother Monty lose their father, a boxer, to accumulated injuries from his sport. The story takes place in a poor inner-city neighborhood near Boston. Monty wants to be a boxer and sneaks away to train. George takes his responsibilities with his younger brother seriously but finally learns how to steer him away from boxing. (7–up)

Myers, Walter Dean. *Handbook for Boys: A Novel.* HarperCollins, 2002. ISBN 0-0602-9146-X

A judge assigns Jimmy Lynch, sixteen years old, to a youth facility for six months. Instead, Duke Wilson, barbershop owner, who has a successful community-mentoring program, offers to take Jimmy into the program. Jimmy comes to the barbershop each day after school to work and listen to life's lessons from Duke and his diverse set of customers. (8–up)

Peters, Julie Anne. *Define "Normal."* Little, Brown and Company, 2000. ISBN 0-316-70631-0
 Antonia and Jazz are about as opposite as two girls can be. Antonia is a peer counselor to Jazz, and gradually they develop a friendship and realize that they are more alike than they thought. (7–10)

 If everyone sweeps in front of his own front door, all the world would be clean.
 —Anonymous

Werlin, Nancy. *The Killer's Cousin.* Bantam Books, 1998. ISBN 0-385-32560-6
 David has just been acquitted of killing his girlfriend, and his family is sending him to live with his aunt and uncle and eleven-year-old Lily. David will repeat his senior year of high school and hopes to get his life back in order. But Lily is intent on harassing and tormenting David. Why is she doing this? Why won't anyone believe David when he says Lily needs help? (9–12)

Wolff, Virginia Euwer. *True Believer.* Atheneum Children's Books, 2001. ISBN 0-689-82827-6
 LaVaughn is fifteen years old; she lives in the projects but is preparing to go to college. She is very loyal to her dad who died a while back, and she finds herself missing him as her mother begins dating. LaVaughs's two best friends are changing and leaving her behind. To make matters worse, Jody moves back to town, and LaVaughn doesn't know what to think. (7–up)

Nonfiction

Adler, David A. *Our Golda: The Story of Golda Meir.* Viking, 1984. ISBN 0-670-53107-3
 Librarian, schoolteacher, shopkeeper, almond picker, and fund-raiser are among the various jobs Golda Meir held. She was one of the great leaders of Israel and its prime minister. (Juvenile)

Bang, Molly. *Nobody Particular: One Woman's Fight to Save the Bays.* Henry Holt, 2001. ISBN 0-8050-5396-4
 As a shrimper and a mother, Diane Wilson thought she was no one in particular. When she learned that she was living in one of the most polluted counties in the United States, she began a campaign to save the Texas bays—the same bays on which her father and grandfather had made their livings. She went up against one of the largest producers of PVC, Formosa Plastics, and forces the company to adopt stricter environmental safeguards in an effort to protect the bays. (4–8)

Clinton, Susan. *Herbert Hoover.* Children's Press, 1988. ISBN 0-516-01355-6
 Herbert Hoover was raised a Quaker and became an orphan at nine years old. He lived with relatives in Oregon. He studied geology in college and became a mining engineer. He traveled the world, started his own company, and became a millionaire. He became president in 1928 just before the country entered the Great Depression. Hoover "clung to his idea that government should help people to help themselves." (5–8)

Fritz, Jean. *You Want Women to Vote, Lizzie Stanton?* G. P. Putnam's Sons, 1995. ISBN 0-399-22786-5
 Lizzie's father wished she were a boy. Lizzie strived to be smart and brave. She eloped because her father did not approve of her choice for a husband. In the wedding ceremony, she would not promise to "obey" her future husband. Elizabeth Cady Stanton promoted equality for all, men and women, black and white. She died in 1902; it would be another eighteen years before women would have the right to vote. (3–7)

McLoone, Margo. *Booker T. Washington.* Bridgestone Books, 1997. ISBN 1-56065-520-8
   Booker T. Washington, an educator, started the Tuskegee Institute in Alabama. He was born a slave in 1856 and freed when he was nine years old. He believed that African Americans should have well-paying jobs and wrote a book titled *Up from Slavery.* "More and more, we must learn to think non in terms of race or color or language or religion or political boundaries, but in terms of humanity." (2–4)

 Provision for others is the fundamental responsibility of human life.
   —Woodrow Wilson

Muskat, Carrie. *Sammy Sousa: Pride of the Dominican Republic.* Mitchell Lane, 2000. ISBN 1-883845-96-3
   Sammy Sousa's father died when he was seven years old, and his mother struggled to raise her family. The children played baseball in the street when they were not busy with chores. Sammy started playing organized ball when he was fourteen years old and signed his first professional contract when he was sixteen. He went on to set and break many records. He has not forgotten his roots and contributes money and computers to schools and ambulances to his homeland. When the Dominican Republic was hit by Hurricane George in 1998, Sammy organized a relief effort to help those who lost everything. (4–8)

Winter, Jeanette. *The Librarian of Basra: A True Story from Iraq.* Harcourt Brace Jovanovich, 2005. ISBN 0-15-205-445-6
   Alia Baker is the librarian in Basra, Iraq. She worried that with the threat of war, the books in the library would not be safe. When war came to Basra, she asked friends, neighbors, and family to help her move the books to a neighboring restaurant. Later on, she moved the books once again to her home and the houses of friends while she waited and dreamed of a new library. (2–4)

Chapter 6

Perseverance

Related Virtues

Self-motivation, self-reliance, persistence, work ethic, industriousness, ambition, resilience, endurance, and self-control

Definition

Steady persistence in adhering to a course of action, a belief, or a purpose; steadfastness

Perseverance in Action

✧ Do not give up when the work or task becomes challenging.

✧ Finish assignments.

✧ Keep practicing.

✧ Stick with the team.

✧ Count to ten when something frustrates you or makes you angry.

✧ Try something new.

✧ Find your talents and develop them.

✧ Work to eliminate bad habits.

✧ Exercise self-control.

People Who Have Demonstrated This Virtue

✧ Lance Armstrong

✧ Sojourner Truth

✧ Harriet Tubman

- ✧ Martin Luther King, Jr.
- ✧ Rosa Parks
- ✧ Wilma Rudolph
- ✧ John Glen
- ✧ Helen Keller
- ✧ Christopher Reeve

Discussion Questions

- ✧ Is perseverance toward a goal always a good thing?
- ✧ When might it be a good idea to give up, or at least make an adjustment to your goal?
- ✧ What are some goals that you have for the future?
- ✧ Do you think someone who is a professional athlete has to have perseverance?
- ✧ Does it take perseverance to get a good education?
- ✧ Why do you suppose people give up?

Related Topics to Explore

- ✧ Pioneers
- ✧ Perseverance mottos
- ✧ Mistakes that worked
- ✧ Climbing Mount Everest
- ✧ Long distance runners or skiers
- ✧ Famous marathon runners
- ✧ The man who broke four-minute mile and other record breakers
- ✧ Explorers and inventors

Annotated Titles

Picture Books

Brimmer, Larry Dane. *The Littlest Wolf.* HarperCollins, 2002. ISBN 0-06-029040-4
   Big Gray has several pups, but one in particular is unable to do the same things that his brother and sisters can do. Big Gray reassures the little wolf that what he does is just fine for his size, and in time he will be able to do all that his siblings do. (ps–3)

Chorao, Kay. *Pig and Crow.* Henry Holt, 2000. ISBN 0-8050-5863-X
   Pig is lonely; Crow knows it and offers magic seeds for the cake Pig just baked. The seeds become pumpkins, and he bakes a pie, then sly Crow offers him a worm. When the worm turns into a butterfly and flies away, Pig is lonely once again, and this time Crow offers him an egg that becomes a Canadian goose. Pig works hard to be patient and caring with the goose. When the goose grows up, he shows Pig the wide world from above. (ps–2)

Egielski, Richard. *Slim and Jim.* HarperCollins, 2002. ISBN 0-06-028352-1

Slim is a rat who meets up with Jim, a good mouse, and together they gang up with their yo-yos against Buster the cat. (K–3)

Haas, Jessie. *Runaway Radish.* Greenwillow Books, 2001. ISBN 0-06-029159-1

Radish, the pony, is happiest when he is teaching the young girls in his care how to ride, fall, and go fast. He has several owners throughout the years, but it is always the same—the girls eventually grow and are too big to ride Radish. One day, lonely Radish gets out and soon is lost; however, he remembers his way back to his original owner. Judy knows that Radish is happiest when doing what he does best: teaching young children how to ride and be brave. Judy convinces the current owner of Radish to let him go to a riding camp where he will always have a constant supply of young children to teach. (2–up)

Henderson, Kathy. *Dog Story.* Bloomsbury, 2004. ISBN 0-7475-7133-3

"Jo wanted a dog more than anything else in the whole wide world." Her parents always say no and substitute other small animals, and even a baby. Nothing satisfies Jo, and when things get out of control, Grandma arrives with a gift of a dog, and all is well. (ps–2)

Martin, Jacqueline Briggs. *Grandmother Bryant's Pocket.* Houghton Mifflin, 1996. ISBN 0-395-68984-8

In the 1700s, pockets were not sewn into a garment but tied around a woman's waist. Sarah is sent to her grandparents for the summer. With the help of her grandmother's pocket and a one-eyed cat, Sarah is able to overcome her fears and nightmares after her dog is killed in a fire. (ps–3)

McMullan, Kate. *Good Night, Stella.* Candlewick Press, 1994. ISBN 1-56402-065-7

Stella is unable to go to sleep so she decides to wait up for her mother who is at the movies. She plays in her room until she is exhausted and falls asleep, then her father tucks her in. (ps–up)

Nickle, John. *The Ant Bully.* Scholastic, 1999. ISBN 0-590-39591-2

Sid, the neighborhood bully, is mean to Lucas, so Lucas, in turn, is mean to ants and squirts them with his squirt gun. When they have had enough, the ants attack Lucas and shrink him to their size. He is put on trial and does hard labor with the worker ants. Lucas toils away, and finally the queen ant has more request for Lucas. He returns to normal size only to face the bully Sid once again. But the ants see Sid first. (ps–2)

Root, Phyllis. *Rattletrap Car.* Candlewick Press, 2001. ISBN 0-7636-0919-6

The family is hot and decides to go to the lake in their rattletrap car. As things keep breaking down on the car, the family repairs the car with the toys and food they have with them. They reach the lake and even make it home again. (ps–2)

Primary (grades 1–3)

Avi. *Prairie School.* HarperCollins, 2001. ISBN 0-06-027664-9

Noah moves with his parents from Maine to a sod house in Colorado in 1880. Noah loves spending time on the prairie, and when his Aunt Dora comes to teach him how to read and write, Noah finds many excuses to avoid learning. Aunt Dora uses the outdoors and the prairie to demonstrate to Noah all the things that he will know once he works hard and learns how to read. (2–4)

Bunting, Eve. *Dandelions.* Harcourt Brace, 1995. ISBN 0-15-200050-X

A family leaves Illinois and slowly makes their way to the Nebraska Territory, where Papa stakes a claim. Zoe and her father go to town to stock up on supplies, and on the way home Zoe sees some dandelions to take home for Mama. They plant the dandelions on the sod roof so that they will be seen from a distance. Mama doubts that they will survive, but Zoe reminds her that the dandelions will bloom because they are strong and determined, just like her family. (K–3)

Byars, Betsy. *Little Horse.* St. Martin's Press, 2001. ISBN 0-8050-6413-3
    One day Little Horse goes to the stream alone and falls in. Little Horse is swiftly carried downstream away from the valley where he was born. After many adventures, Little Horse is picked up and placed securely and safely in a pocket and taken to the land of big horses. Little Horse is given to a smaller animal that places Little Horse in his own special cave of wood, with water to drink and oats to eat. Little Horse feels safe and dreams of the journey he will make some day back to his home and valley. (1–3)

Genius is divine perseverance. Genius I cannot claim nor even extra brightness but perseverance all can have.
—Woodrow Wilson

Hinton, S. E. *The Puppy Sister.* Delacorte Press, 1995. ISBN 0-385-32060-4
    When Nick receives his new puppy, he says that he would rather have a sister. Aleasha, the puppy, over time complies with Nick's wishes. Gradually she changes into his sister, with ears a little too pointed and teeth a little too sharp. (2–3)

Lester, Julius. *John Henry.* Puffin Picture, 1999. ISBN 0-14-056622-8
    This story is a retelling of an African American tale about a man with unusual strength who challenges, with perseverance, a steam drill digging through mountains. The dramatic climax of the story is set at the time of the building of the railroad through the Allegheny Mountains in West Virginia. A Caldecott Honor Book. (K–5)

McGill, Alice. *Molly Bannaky.* Houghton Mifflin, 1999. ISBN 0-395-72287-X
    Benjamin Banneker was a respected scientist and mathematician in the late 1700s. This is the story of his grandmother, who came to America as an indentured servant and orphan at the age of seventeen. After seven years of hard work, Molly is free to stake her claim on land in the wilderness. The farm becomes too much for a woman alone, so she buys a regal black slave and vows to free him. They fall in love, and Molly, a white woman, breaks colonial law when she marries Bannaky. They have four daughters, and when Bannaky dies, Molly and her daughters work their hundred acres. In time, Molly teaches her grandson, Benjamin, how to read and write and about his grandfather, the son of a king in Africa. (ps–03)

Park, Barbara. *Junie B. Jones Is Captain Field Day.* Random House, 2001. ISBN 0-375-90291-0
    Junie B. Jones draws the slip that makes her captain of her class's field day. Junie is the only one who claps when she draws her own name. Junie thinks she should now be the superhero, the one who keeps the team united, not just a supporter of the team. Junie finally puts her faith in weak William, who rises to the challenge and wins the pull-ups, the day, and Junie's cape. (00–2)

Rylant, Cynthia. *Henry and Mudge and the Careful Cousin.* Bradbury Press, 1994. ISBN 0-02-778021-X
    Henry and his dog, Mudge, are waiting for Annie, a cousin Henry has never met. When she arrives, Henry is worried because she is so neat and clean and doesn't want anything to do with Mudge, especially his kisses. Henry keeps trying to find something that they can both enjoy and do without upsetting Annie. Finally he tries playing Frisbee, and both are amazed that Annie is good at it. Annie forgets about staying neat and clean, and together they have a good time. (00–3)

Thomas, Shelley Moore. *Good Night, Good Knight*. Dutton Children's Books, 2000. ISBN 0-525-46326-7

This is the story of three lonely little dragons that live in a dark cave and need some help going to sleep. The Good Knight comes from his tower each time a dragon roars and gives one a drink of water, reads a story to another, and sings a song to the third. He no sooner gets back to the tower when he hears yet another roar louder than all before and once again goes to see what the dragons want. This time they all want a good night kiss from the Good Knight. (ps–2)

Intermediate (grades 3–5)

Christopher, Matt. *Snowboard Maverick*. Little, Brown and Company, 1997. ISBN 0-316-14203-4

Skateboarding has been Dennis's passion since he was eight years old. He is the best in town and loves his sport seven months of the year. During the winter when his friends are snowboarding, Dennis stays away from the slopes. When he was seven years old, he had a bad skiing accident and is now afraid to try snowboarding. His friends encourage Dennis to try because it is so similar to skateboarding. Dennis likes his new sport and knows that he is a newbie but allows Rick Hogan to dare him to race down Ford Mountain. In one year, Dennis overcomes his fears and learns the sport. (4–7)

 Great works are performed not by strength, but by perseverance.
—Samuel Johnson

_____. *Soccer Scoop*. Little, Brown and Company, 1998. ISBN 0-316-14206-9

Mac loves soccer and is a good athlete with a big mouth. He is the goalie on the team and is known to chatter at the players during the game. Mac changes his upbeat attitude on and off the field when critical cartoons about him begin to appear in the school newspaper. Who is behind it? Could it be one of his own teammates? (3–5)

Coville, Bruce. *Song of the Wanderer*. Scholastic, 1999. ISBN 0-590-45953-8

This is the second book of the Unicorn Chronicles Trilogy, and although the first book is briefly summarized, the adventures in this book will be better understood if the first book has been read. Cara, an earth girl who has become the protector of the unicorns in Luster, is told by the queen to find her grandmother, the Wanderer. Her quest is filled with secret caves, strange creatures, and rainbow prisons. The ending is left open with a threat of a final battle between the unicorns and the hunters that will decide the fate of the unicorns. (3–7)

Kehret, Peg. *My Brother Made Me Do It*. Pocket Star, 2000. ISBN 0-671-03418-9

Julie Welsh, a fifth grader, has taken a pen pal as part of a class project. Mrs. Kaplan, who lives in Kansas, is eighty-nine years old and has cancer. Julie is diagnosed with juvenile arthritis, but her mischievous younger brother prods her to run in a fund-raising race. Despite her illness, and with the encouragement of Mrs. Kaplan, Julie makes a commitment and shows amazing determination to get on with her life. (4–6)

Krensky, Stephen. *Arthur and the Scare-Your-Pants-Off Club*. Little, Brown and Company, 1998. ISBN 0-316-11548-7

Arthur is in a hurry to go to the library to get the new book in the Scare-Your-Pants-Off Club series. When he arrives, his friends are there when the librarian announces that all the books in the SYPOC series are removed from the shelf. PAWS, or Parents against Weird Stories, object to the books and have them removed. Arthur and his friends initiate a petition to have the books put back on the shelf. (3–up)

Osborne, Mary Pope. *The One-Eyed Giant, Book One.* Hyperion, 2002. ISBN 0-7868-0770-9

Odysseus, from the island of Ithaca, is called to join King Agamemnon in the fight against Troy. For ten years, they camp outside the wall of Troy until the Goddess Athena reveals to Odysseus her plan to build a wooden horse to house Greek soldiers. The Trojans bring the wooden horse into the city, and under the cover of darkness the Greek soldiers open the gates to their fellow warriors. By dawn, the city is in flames. Thus begins the journey of Odysseus back to Ithaca and his beloved family. (3–6)

Middle School (grades 5–8)

Bartoletti, Susan Campbell. *A Coal Miner's Bride.* Scholastic, 2000. ISBN 0-439-05386-2

Anetka leaves her home in Poland and joins up with her father in America. She is betrothed to Stanley, a widower with three young girls. Anetka does not want to be a coal miner's wife, but she tries. Stanley dies in a coal-mining accident, and Anetka is forced to take in borders. Among them is Leon, whom she knew and liked in the old country. Eventually Anetka finds true happiness with Leon, marries him, and they have a daughter. (4–9)

Clements, Andrew. *Things Not Seen.* Philomel, 2002. ISBN 0-399-23626-0

Ever wonder what it would be like to be invisible? One morning, Bobby wakes up and discovers he is invisible. Now he cannot do anything the way he did before. His situation becomes complicated when his parents are hospitalized from a car accident. What if this is a permanent situation? Will his life be like this forever? Bobby makes a decision not to wait around for stuff to happen to him. He perseveres and makes the most of his life, beginning with a relationship with a blind girl, Alicia, who helps him figure out a solution to his invisibility. (6–up)

Ellis, Deborah. *Mud City.* Douglas & McIntyre, 2003. ISBN 0-88899-518-0

Shauzia is a refugee from Afghanistan with dreams of going to the sea and sailing to France. Shauzia and her dog, Jasper, are at the Widow's Compound for women and children in Pakistan. She chaffs at the conditions, lack of privacy, and orders from Mrs. Weera. She disguises herself as a boy, leaves the safety of the camp, and walks to Peshawar, a major city. Life is hard; oftentimes Shauzia and Jasper are hungry, but she manages to save some money, which is taken away from her when she is arrested. Shauzia is rescued from jail, and she ends up back at the Widow's Compound, but with perseverance, she faces her life there with a different attitude. (5–7)

Gregory, Kristiana. *The Winter of Red Snow: The Revolutionary War Diary of Abigail Jane Stewart.* Scholastic, 1996. ISBN 0-590-22653-3

Abigail Jane Stewart lives near Valley Forge, Pennsylvania, and writes in her diary about the conditions, hardships, and sufferings of the Continental Army in 1777–1778. The epilogue tells what happens to the fictional characters and the historical note describes life in this time period. (4–9)

Hamilton, Virginia. *Bluish.* Blue Sky Press, 1999. ISBN 0-439-36786-7

This book follows the growing friendship between Dreenie, Tuli, and Natalie. Natalie is in a wheelchair and recovering from leukemia. She is called Bluish because of the color of her skin from all the chemotherapy she undergoes. The narrative is interspersed with journal entries written by Dreenie with observations about Bluish, her illness, and their relationship. (4–9)

Kimmel, Elizabeth Cody. *Visiting Miss Caples.* Dial Books for Young Readers, 2000. ISBN 0-8037-2502-7

The service project for the year is to visit an elderly person weekly. When Jen visits Miss Caples, she cannot get a reaction of any sort for the whole hour. At first, Jen reads to her, and then she talks to her about her problems at school and with her best friend, Liv. Jen adores her lively, beautiful, and popular friend, but she is noticing that Liv can be very cruel to those who cross her. After many visits, Miss Caples finally begins to talk to Jen and tells her about a similar relationship she had with her best friend when she was at a boarding school. Miss Caples warns Jen that Liv may be dangerous and gives Jen the impetus and strength to break off their friendship. (5–9)

Park, Linda Sue. *A Single Shard*. Clarion Books, 2001. ISBN 0-395-97827-0
A Single Shard is a humble story of perseverance, patience, and courage. The story takes place during the twelfth century in a potter's village in Korea. Tree-ear is orphaned at a young age and brought to the village of Ch'ulp'o to live with an uncle. When he arrives, the uncle dies of the fever, and Tree-ear is brought to Crane-man who is to take care of him. Tree-ear remains with Crane-man, and they live under the bridge surviving by their wiles and frugalness. Tree-ear is fascinated by the potter, Min, and observes him unbeknownst to Min. One day when Tree-ear is bold enough to pick up one of the unfired pieces, Min startles him, and the boy drops the piece. Tree-ear shows courage and strength by working long and hard to repay his debt to Min in the hopes of becoming a potter one day. (5–9)

YA (grades 8–12)

Barrett, Tracy. *Anna of Byzantium*. Bantam Doubleday Dell Books, 1999. ISBN 0-440-41536-5
Anna Comnena expects to inherit the Byzantium throne in the eleventh century. The story begins with Anna at seventeen, when she is exiled to a convent after she attempts to assassinate her younger brother to keep him from the throne. Her brother, John, perseveres and eventually does inherit the throne. He becomes one of the most beloved Byzantium emperors, while Anna becomes a scholar and writes an eleven-book epic about the life of her father. (6–10)

 Life is not easy for any of us. But what of that? We must have perseverance and above all confidence in ourselves. We must believe that we are gifted for something and that this thing must be attained.
—Marie Curie

Bruchac, Joseph. *Code Talker: A Novel about the Navajo Marines of World War Two*. Dial Books for Young Readers, 2005. ISBN 0-8037-2921-9
At an early age, Joe is chosen to leave his family and go to school to learn the ways and language of the white man. In the process, his long hair is cut, his Navajo clothes and decorations are taken away, and he is forbidden to use his native language. Joe is able to adjust easier than other Native Americans, and soon he surprises his teachers with his intelligence. When he is fifteen years old, the Japanese bomb Pearl Harbor, and the Native Americans are actively recruited. Joe enlists in the Marines and is asked to participate in a secret operation. Much to his surprise, his ability to communicate in both English and Navajo is prized and encouraged. After a few weeks of training, Joe is sent to the Pacific as a Navajo code talker. He is only seventeen years old, yet he is in the middle of a war with many adventures ahead. (5–up)

Cushman, Karen. *The Midwife's Apprentice*. Clarion Books, 1995. ISBN 0-395-69229-6
This story takes place in medieval England. Alyce rises from homelessness and namelessness to become an apprentice to an old midwife, Jane Sharp. (7–up)

Dygard, Thomas J. *River Danger*. HarperCollins, 1998. ISBN 0-688-14852-2
Eric, eighteen years old, and his brother Robbie, eleven years old, are on a canoe trip when they meet up with a group of car thieves. Eric is held hostage and must rely on Robbie to rescue him. Robbie finds his way through the wilderness to a road and stops a car to get help. He shows perseverance and daring in rescuing his older brother. (7–12)

Levine, Gail Carson. *Ella Enchanted.* HarperCollins, 1997. ISBN 0-06-027510-3

This is a type of Cinderella story, but it is not really clear that this is the case until near the end of the book. Ella is visited by a fairy as a baby and given the gift of obedience, which turns out to be a curse. Ella must obey every command given to her, and she cannot refuse. Ella becomes friends with Prince Char at a young age. Ella's mother dies when Ella is still young, and her father sends her off to finishing school. The two daughters of an acquaintance go along and the older girl discovers Ella's curse and make Ella her personal slave. Ella runs away from school and makes her way home. Then her romance with Prince Char begins with a true "Cinderella" ending. (3–up)

Myers, Walter Dean. *The Glory Field.* Scholastic, 1994. ISBN 0-590-45897-3

This is an in-depth look at the Lewis family, African Americans who continually struggle for freedom and equality. These stories show how each generation takes a stand against oppression and how slow and costly the process is. (7–9)

Napoli, Donna Jo. *Daughter of Venice.* Delacorte Press, 2002. ISBN 0-385-32780-3

Donata is fourteen years old, and her future is uncertain. She is the younger daughter of a wealthy nobleman, and only the eldest daughter in the family will marry. Donata wants to be educated like her brothers and explore Venice freely. The only way she will be able to do this is by sneaking out of her house disguised as a boy. She proves to be an excellent student and has many experiences on the streets of Venice. (7–10)

Fall seven times, stand up eight.
    —Japanese Proverb

Patterson, James. *Maximum Ride: The Angel Experiment.* Little, Brown and Company, 2005. ISBN 0-316-15556-X

Max (short for Maximum) is a fourteen-year-old girl and the leader of a group of orphans who have escaped from the institution where they were created. They are 98 percent human and 2 percent bird; they have wings and can fly. Mutants called Erasers who want the orphans back at the lab are chasing them. The mutants do manage to capture the youngest one, Angel, and so Max and the rest work together to get her back. (6–up)

Paulsen, Gary. *Sarny: A Life Remembered.* Delacorte Press, 1997. ISBN 0-385-32195-3

This is a sequel to *Nightjohn*. After the two of Sarny's children are sold into slavery and her husband is worked to death, Sarny searches for and finds her children in New Orleans. Sarny remarries and perseveres in teaching black children how to read and write. (6–9)

_____. *Transall Saga.* Delacorte Press, 1998. ISBN 0-385-32196-1

Mark is on his first hiking trip when a mysterious blue light transports him to a thick jungle world of beasts, romance, and slavery. He shows perseverance and determination to get back home again. It is then that he realizes that the time warp is actually a glimpse of the future world. (7–12)

Nonfiction

Adler, David A. *A Picture Book of Helen Keller.* Holiday House, 1990. ISBN 0-8234-0818-3

This is a brief narrative about Helen Keller who became deaf and blind after a childhood illness. Anne Sullivan was hired as her teacher and helped her to understand words that were signed on her hand and to read Braille. She learned to speak and went to college with Anne Sullivan at her side. Helen Keller became an inspiration to deaf and blind people and was given the Presidential Medal of Freedom. (ps–3)

Armstrong, Kristin. *Lance Armstrong: The Race of His Life.* Penguin Putnam Books for Young Readers, 2000. ISBN 0-448-42407-X

Lance Armstrong received his first bike when he was seven. He lived in Plano, Texas, with his mother, who was always by his side. Lance won races all over the United Stated and went to Italy when he was eighteen to train. In his first race in Europe, Lance came in last. That only made him train harder by riding in the mountains. At twenty-one years old, Lance Armstrong became the youngest person to win the world championship. Lance continued to win races, including the Tour de France, but when he turned twenty-five, he discovered that he had a bigger race to win—a race against cancer. Cancer spread throughout his body, even to his brain. He was operated on and took cancer-fighting drugs until he was cancer free. He started riding and asking teams to take a chance with him. Only the U.S. Postal Service Cycling Team would take a chance. He went on to win the Tour de France seven times. (4–7)

Bartoletti, Susan Campbell. *Growing Up in Coal Country.* Houghton Mifflin, 1996. ISBN 0-395-77847-6

Oral history and archival documents are used to piece together the story of children's lives in the coal country of northeastern Pennsylvania during the nineteenth and twentieth centuries. Many of the children were immigrants, and the boys were passed off as fourteen years old and put to work even though they might have been younger. Black-and-white photos and the narrative tell the story. (4–7)

_____. *Kids on Strike!* Houghton Mifflin, 1999. ISBN 0-395-88892-1

Children can make a difference. The author traces the working conditions and the steps children took to bolster their civil rights in the nineteenth and twentieth centuries. Black-and-white photographs document their contributions and arduous journey. (4–7)

Burford, Betty. *Chocolate by Hershey.* Carolrhoda Books, 1994. ISBN 0-87614-830-5

Milton Hershey was born in 1857 to Mennonite parents. The Mennonites are hardworking, peace-loving people. Young Milton loved his parents, but he knows that he can never be as serious as his mother. When he was thirteen years old, he began to learn the trade of candy making, and at eighteen he moved to Philadelphia to start his own business. It was a bumpy road and Milton moved around but did not give up. He returned home to start a candy business, which becomes Milton Hershey's Lancaster Caramel Company. (3–6)

Connoly, Sean. *Nelson Mandela: An Unauthorized Biography.* Heinemann Library, 2000. ISBN 1-57572-225-9

South Africa denied basic human rights to non-whites through its policy of apartheid. Nelson Mandela spent thirty years in prison to promote a change in policy. Through his determination and perseverance, Nelson led his country after his release from prison and made it a better place for all. (5–7)

Cooper, Floyd. *Jump! From the Life of Michael Jordan.* Philomel Books, 2004. ISBN 0-399-24230-9

Michael Jordan's first opponent as a child was his older brother, Larry. Often he stayed out past dinner and practiced until his father called him to bed. He tried out for the high school basketball team and did not make the cut but continued to play junior varsity. He practiced every morning before school, and eventually a champion was made. (5–up)

Cummings, Pat, and Linda Cummings. *Talking with Adventurers.* National Geographic Society, 1998. ISBN 0-395-88892-1

Each of the twelve adventurers featured in this book loves his or her work and faces many obstacles and hardships along the way. They describe how they become "interested in the subject that became a life's work," and each answers the same ten questions. Included are the following adventurers: Christina M. Allen (rain forest ecologist), Robert Ballard (explorer), Michael L. Blakey (anthropologist), Ann Bowles (bioacoustician), David Doubilet (underwater photographer), Jane Googall (ethologist), Dereck and Beverly Joubert (wildlife filmmakers), Michael Novacek (paleontologist), Johan Reinhard (anthropologist), Rick C. West (arachnologist), and Juris Zarins (archaeologist). (4–7)

Fritz, Jean. *Bully for You, Teddy Roosevelt.* G. P. Putnam's Sons, 1991. ISBN 0-399-21769-X
 Teddy Roosevelt was sickly as a youth and schooled at home by tutors. His father encouraged Teddy to exercise and build his body because the boy was prone to asthma. No matter what Teddy took on, he gave his all—and then some. He never wanted to disappoint his father. Teddy went on to write books, create his own Museum of Natural History, become governor of New York, and then vice president and finally president of the United States. He was a dynamo in all he did. (5–9)

Kramer, Barbara. *Trailblazing American Women: First in Their Fields.* Enslow, 2000. ISBN 0-7660-1377-4
 The ten women in this book are motivated to succeed in their careers and make history by being the first in their fields. They represent a variety of professions and time periods. The ten women profiled are as follows: Jane Addams (winner of the Nobel Peace Prize), Madam C. J. Walker (businesswoman), Harriet Quimby (aviator), Jeannette Rankin (congresswoman), Frances Perkins (secretary of labor), Pearl S. Buck (winner of Nobel Prize in Literature), Althea Gibson (tennis champion), Sandra Day O'Connor (U.S. Supreme Court Justice), Marlene Sanders (newswoman), and Antonia C. Novello (U.S. surgeon general). (6–12)

Lawlor, Laurie. *Helen Keller: Rebellious Spirit.* Holiday House, 2001. ISBN 0-8234-1588-0
 Helen lost her sight and hearing when she was nineteen months old. When she was ten years old and spoke, she was celebrated and recognized worldwide for her accomplishments. She was able to function normally in a talking world because of her sense of humor, energy, and a rebellious, sometimes stubborn, spirit. (5–up)

 Perseverance is patience concentrated.
 —Thomas Carlyle

McCheon, Marc. *The Kid Who Named Pluto and the Stories of Other Extraordinary Young People in Science.* Chronicle Books, 2004. ISBN 0-8118-3770-X
 This is the story of famous and not-so-famous young boys and girls who pursue their ideas and dreams. Their stories are told with many illustrations and photographs. They include Robert Goddard, Venetia Burney, Isaac Asimov, Philo Taylor Farnsworth, Mary Anning, Sarah Flannery, Truman Henry Safford, Emily Rosa, and Louis Braille. (3–6)

Olesky, Walter. *Christopher Reeve.* Lucent Books, 2000. ISBN 1-56006-534-6
 Before Christopher Reeve's horseback riding injury, which left him a quadriplegic, he was a movie star and social and political activist. After the accident, he returned to motion picture directing and became an advocate for spinal cord injury research and victims of paralysis. (5–9)

Porter, A. P. *Jump at de Sun: The Story of Zora Neale Hurston.* Carolrhoda Books, 1992. ISBN 0-87614-667-1
 Zora Neale Hurston was born in 1891, in Eatonville, Florida, near Orlando. She was the last of five children, and her father never let her forget his disappointment that she was a girl. Zora's mother, Lucy, taught all of her children to "jump for the sun"—they might not make it, but at least they would get off the ground. Lucy died when Zora was thirteen years old. Zora met prejudice for

the first time when she left Eatonville for Jacksonville. She spent many years wandering, attending school, living in Harlem, and writing and collecting African American tales. Zora wrote four novels, two books of folklore, and an autobiography, as well as articles, essays, short stories, and plays. (4–7)

Ringgold, Faith. *My Dream of Martin Luther King.* Crown Publishers, New York, 1995. ISBN 0-517-59976-7

Young Faith has a dream about Martin Luther King's life. In the beginning, people of all ages and colors are bringing their bags of hate and prejudice to trade in for freedom, hope, and peace. The dream continues to relive the important events in Martin's life until his death, at which time the bags of hate and prejudice are being exchanged for the hero's dream. (00–3)

St. George, Judith. *You're on Your Way, Teddy Roosevelt.* Philomel Books, 2004. ISBN 0-399-23888-3

Young Teddy Roosevelt was always sickly with asthma, and his parents tried everything to keep him well. They spent the summer in the country, traveled to Europe for a year, even gave him "coffee to drink and cigars to smoke to help his breathing." He remained puny and ill. One day a doctor suggested exercises to expand his lungs. Teddy enrolled in a gym, took boxing lessons, and proceeded to build up his body while participating in sports. This did not cure his illness, "but he was determined to control his asthma and illnesses rather than letting his asthma and illnesses control him." (5–up)

Schwager, Tina. *Gutsy Girls: Young Women Who Dare.* Free Spirit, 1999. ISBN 1-57542-059-7

This book profiles twenty-five young women who have a passion for what they do and have overcome—"obstacles, limitations, fears, doubts, losses, and tests of their physical and mental endurance." Those featured include a college football player, an ocean sailor, a skydiver, a mountain climber, a drag racer, a circus performer, a kick boxer, and an Antarctic researcher. Part two offers help on getting the mind and body in shape and lists women and girls who have contributed to history through the feats they accomplished. (6–12)

Winter, Jonah. *Frida.* Arthur A. Levine Books, 2002. ISBN 0-590-20320-7

Frida Kahlo was a world-renowned Mexican painter. This is a brief story of her life and the obstacles she overcame daily. When she was seven years old, she was stricken with polio and left with a shrunken left leg and a limp. When she was eighteen, she was in a terrible accident that left her in constant pain. In both instances, it was her art that saw her through. "She turns her pain into something beautiful." (ps–4)

Chapter 7

Loyalty

Related Virtues

Commitment, faithfulness, steadfastness, obedience, and dependability

Definition

A feeling or attitude of devoted attachment and affection

Loyalty in Action

◇ Support your school teams.

◇ Show school spirit.

◇ Participate in volunteer work and community service projects.

◇ Always do your best for your school.

◇ Arrive on time for classes, activities, and sports.

◇ Participate in activities.

◇ Follow the school rules.

◇ Follow through on commitments to your school.

◇ In group and team work, do your share.

People Who Have Demonstrated This Virtue

◇ Arnold Palmer

◇ Ernest Hemingway

◇ Robert E. Lee

◇ Joe Paterno

♦ Haile Selassie I

♦ Sir Winston Churchill

♦ Abraham Lincoln

♦ Johann Sebastian Bach

♦ Nancy Reagan

♦ Gerald Ford

Discussion Questions

♦ Should you be loyal to someone, no matter what?

♦ Describe a character who displays loyalty from a book you have read.

♦ What criteria should you use to determine whether your loyalty is wise?

♦ Do you keep promises?

♦ Do you expect your friends and family to follow through for you?

♦ What are some pledges of loyalty that people make?

♦ Why is loyalty important?

♦ Are you dependable?

♦ Why is it important to be faithful to your beliefs?

Related Topics to Explore

♦ Examples of loyalty in history

♦ Examples of civil disobedience

♦ Symbols that inspire loyalty

♦ Dog obedience training

♦ Sports loyalty

♦ Guide dogs

♦ Characteristics of leadership

Annotated Titles

Picture Books

Asch, Frank. *The Earth and I.* Harcourt Brace, 1994. ISBN 0-15-200443-2
    A small boy has a relationship with the earth. When the earth is happy, he is happy; but when the earth is sad, the boy is sad. He is friends with the earth and loyal to the environment. (ps–3)

Namioka, Lensey. *The Loyal Cat.* Harcourt Children's Books, 1995. ISBN 0-15-200092-5
    A priest at a mountain temple in northern Japan rescues a kitten. The priest is satisfied with his humble life but becomes so poor that he must even beg for food. The kitten wants a better life, so he uses his magical powers at a royal funeral and puts the priest in the position to win lots of gold. The priest is satisfied with enough gold to repair the temple and live comfortably, but the cat sometimes thinks about the things they could have had. (ps–3)

Ormerod, Jan. *Emily and Albert.* Chronicle, 2004. ISBN 0-8118-3615-0

Emily and Albert are friends, and they share a lot—they smell things, have the hiccups, dance, feel better, and read a book in five easy-to-read chapters. (ps–2)

Santiago, Chiori. *Home to Medicine Mountain.* Children's Book Press, 1998. ISBN 0-89239-155-3

Based on a true story, two American Indian boys leave the pine woods of Medicine Mountain to go to a boarding school a long way from home. They are given uniforms and warned only to speak English, especially in front of the teachers. In the summer, the boys long to go home but learn that the school only pays for them to come to school, not to return home. The boys slip away in the middle of the night and tie themselves to the top of a train on its way back to Medicine Mountain. They return to the school eventually and don't mind it nearly so much because now they have a way back home. (K–3)

Schroeder, Alan. *Minty: A Story of Young Harriet Tubman.* Dial Books for Young Readers, 1996. ISBN 0-8037-1888-8

This is a fictional account of the early life of Harriet Tubman. The basic facts are true; Harriet is considered a difficult slave and is sent to work in the fields. After time, she is becomes a dependable worker. At age twenty-nine, she leaves the Brodas plantation and successfully makes her way to Philadelphia. (K–3)

Primary (grades 1–3)

Brewster, Patience. *Too Many Puppies.* Scholastic, 1997. ISBN 0-590-60276-4

Milly has seven puppies, and at first the little girl wants to keep them all. When the puppies get older, she realizes that seven is too many puppies. She remembers when she received Milly and thinks the one puppy that has grown up is the best of all. (00–2)

Greene, Stephanie. *Owen Foote, Soccer Star.* Clarion Books, 1998. ISBN 0-395-86143-8

This is a sequel to *Owen Foote, Second Grade Strongman.* Owen joins the town soccer league and insists that his best friend, Joseph, sign up, too. It doesn't matter that Joseph has never played soccer and cannot run or kick! When the team bully picks on Joseph, Owen does not stand up for his friend, but when the coach wants to divide the team by skill levels, Owen jumps into action. Owen shows his loyalty to his friend, and they discover that Joseph is an excellent goalie. (1–3)

Hurwitz, Johanna. *PeeWee's Tale.* SeaStar Books, 2000. ISBN 1-58717-028-0

Robbie wants a puppy but receives a hamster from his uncle instead, and he names it Pee-Wee. His mother is horrified that they have a rodent in the house. One day when Robbie is away at a friend's house, his father takes Pee-Wee to a nearby park and lets him go. Pee-Wee is not an ordinary hamster; his mother taught him to read. It comes in handy when he lets his friend, Lexi the squirrel, know that his home is to be chopped down to clear the way for a new playground. Pee-Wee is enjoying his new freedom and friends and has a decision to make when he overhears Robbie's conversation one day in the park. (2–5)

Willner-Pardo, Gina. *When Jane-Marie Told My Secret.* Clarion Books, 1995. ISBN 0-395-66382-2

Jane-Marie is Carolyn's best friend since preschool until the day Carolyn finds out that Jane-Marie told her secret. Carolyn is very upset, and her mother tells her that sometimes even best friends must take a break from each other. Carolyn renews old friendships, and in time the two girls get back together. (ps–3)

Yolen, Jane. *King Long Shanks.* Sagebrush Educational Resources, 2002. ISBN 0-613-53827-7

King Long Shanks, a frog, has very nice legs, and two visiting tailors propose to make new pants for him. They show him a special cloth that will allow the king to see who is loyal to him. The tailors spend many days sewing the cloth that is not there for the summer parade. The big day comes, and King Long Shanks puts on the invisible pants and marches in the parade until a young lad speaks up and says, "King Long Shanks has no pants on!" The queen takes part of her gown and covers the king. "Moral: True loyalty cannot be measured as simply as cloth. But it covers a lot more than legs." (K–4)

Intermediate (grades 3–5)

Avi. *The Good Dog*. Atheneum Books for Young Readers, 2001. ISBN 0-689-83824-7
McKinley is a Malamute and head dog of Steamboat Springs. This story is told from McKinley's point of view. When the greyhound, Duchess, runs away from her owner who mistreats her, it is McKinley who must protect her in hiding. But what is he going to do about Lupin, a wolf, who has come to meet his pack and to try to get the dogs to join up with him. Lupin tells McKinley, "you could become a great dog. You could lead your whole pack to their liberation." (3–6)

Choldenko, Gennifer. *Al Capone Does My Shirts*. G. P. Putnam's Sons, 2004. ISBN 0-399-23861-1
Moose's sister, Natalie, needs to attend a special school in San Francisco. His family moves to Alcatraz where his father works as an electrician and guard. Moose's mother teaches music lessons, which leaves Natalie, who unbeknownst to them is autistic, in Moose's care. After school, Moose takes Natalie outside, and she is accepted by the kids in the small community. Moose relies on instinct, helps his sister, and asks a favor of the famous inmate, Al Capone. (3–6)

Farrell, Mame. *Marrying Malcolm Murgatroyd*. Farrar, Straus & Giroux, 1995. ISBN 0-374-34838-3
Twelve-year-old Hannah has a third-grade brother named Ian who has muscular dystrophy and has been recently confined to a wheelchair. Ian's most supportive friend is Malcolm, a sixth-grade classmate of Hannah's, but more important the son of her parents' best friends. Both sets of parents have been predicting the marriage of Hannah and Malcolm since they were babies. This is a problem for Hannah, because at school she is very cool and Malcolm is a nerd, and Hannah totally ignores him. In the end, she is forced to take a closer look at Malcolm and the values of loyalty and friendship. (4–6)

Hughes, Dean. *Re-elect Nutty!* Atheneum Children's Books, 1995. ISBN 0-689-31862-6
As a fifth grader, Nutty is elected student council president and does the worst job in the school's history. He's now in sixth grade and wants to try again. Nutty plans to run an honest and ethical campaign. Archrival Mindy is running against him, and soon someone is distributing flyers that say rotten things about Nutty. Nutty remains loyal to his goals to the end. (4–7)

Rocklin, Joanne. *Strudel Stories*. Delacorte Press, 1997. ISBN 0-385-32602-5
Grandpa has just died, and Lori and Jessica decide that the way to keep their grandfather's memory alive is to bake the family's strudel recipe and tell the stories he used to tell. Thus begins the telling of seven generations of stories. (3–7)

Spinelli, Jerry. *Crash*. Alfred A. Knopf, 1996. ISBN 0-679-87957-9
John Coogan is a football jock. Crash is his nickname. Penn Webb, a Quaker, is his neighbor and the target of his jokes and pranks. Crash begins to have compassion for Penn after his grandfather's illness. He ends up supporting Penn as he runs in an important race. The common bond between the boys is their love for their grandparents. (3–9)

Middle School (grades 5–8)

Avi. *The Christmas Rat.* Scholastic, 2000. ISBN 0-689-83842-5

Eric's Christmas vacation is looking bad—both his parents work long hours, and his friends are either away or have the flu. His parents ask him to stay at the apartment one day because the exterminator has called to say he will be there. The exterminator turns out to be a strange guy, Anjela Gabrail, ex-military (Special Forces), who uses poisons and a small deadly crossbow with pleasure as he takes his battle against vermin to the extreme. (5–8)

_____. *Crispin: The Cross of Lead.* Hyperion, 2002. ISBN 0-7868-0828-4

When Asta dies, her son, Crispin, a serf and bound to the land, goes into the forest to grieve. When the steward of the manor discovers him, he declares Crispin a "wolf's head," which means that he may be killed on sight. Crispin escapes, but his enemies continue to follow him. The clue to his heritage lies in the lead cross that belonged to his mother and was inscribed by her. This is a mystery to Crispin because he cannot read and didn't know that his mother could read and write. Who are his mother and father, and why is he being pursued? Will the juggler he meets teach him all that he needs to be safe? A Newbery Medal winner. (3–7)

 Equal laws protecting equal rights . . . the best guarantee of loyalty and love of country.
—James Madison

Branford, Henrietta. *Fire, Bed & Bone.* Candlewick Press, 1998. ISBN 0-7636-0338-4

The setting of this historical fiction book is in medieval England and is told from the point of view of a loyal old hunting hound. He lives with his kind master, a serf named Rufus, and his wife, Comfort, who are taken prisoner for attending revolutionary meetings during the Peasant Revolt in 1381. The old dog rescues the children and sees to it that they are safe. When his master is taken prisoner, the cruelty of the times is demonstrated by how the dog and Rufus are both treated. (5–9)

DeFelice, Cynthia. *Lostman's River.* Atheneum Children's Books, 1994. ISBN 0-02-726466-1

This is the story of Tyler and his family, who flee from New York when his father is accused of killing a man. They make their home in the Florida swamp and remain secluded for more than six years until they become involved with the illegal killing of birds for plumes, a practice that is going on all around them. The author makes a plea for the plight of the Everglades. (7–up)

Hobbs, Will. *Wild Man Island.* HarperCollins, 2002. ISBN 0-06-029810-3

Andy sneaks away from his kayak group in the middle of the night in search of Hidden Falls, the spot where his father, an archeologist, died. Andy thinks he can see the falls and return to camp in time for the float plane, scheduled to pick up the group. Returning to camp, Andy is caught in a gale and is forced to land on the Fortress of the Bears or Admiralty Island. Trying to survive, Andy locates an abandoned canning factory and briefly encounters a wild man. Andy asks for help, and the man leaves a spear and flint knife for his protection. A Newfoundland dog is attracted to the smells from the spear and leads Andy to the wild man's survivalist lodgings. Andy has an opportunity to leave the island with the wildlife biologists who are there to trap the wild man's dog so that it doesn't mate with the wolves. Knowing what the biologists are planning to do, Andy escapes and warns the wild man of their plans. Together they leave the island, each with his own plans for the future. (5–up)

Holt, Kimberly Willis. *Dancing in Cadillac Light*. G. P. Putnam's Sons, 2001. ISBN 0-3992-3402-0
    In a poor Texas town in the summer of 1968, eleven-year-old Jaynell Lambert's family must make a big adjustment. Her recently widowed grandfather has come to live with them. His actions lead the family to believe that he is becoming senile. He buys an old emerald-green Cadillac and secretly allows Jaynell to drive it in the fields outside of town. But it surprises his family greatly when he gives the very poor Pickens family his vacant homestead. Grandpop dies suddenly, and the family is devastated to learn that he left everything to the Pickens family—and, more important, the reason why. (5–8)

_____. *My Louisiana Sky*. Henry Holt, 1998. ISBN 0-8050-5251-8
    "Your momma may have a simple mind, Tiger; but her love is simple too. It flows from her like a quick, easy river." Tiger isn't sure when she first became aware of other people's reaction to her mother and father. Both of her parents are mentally deficient. However, Tiger's granny is very strong and sensible and keeps the family together. What will happen when Granny dies? Will Tiger get her wish and leave the small Louisiana town and live with Aunt Dorie Kay? Through it all, Tiger will grow up a little faster and wiser. (5–9)

Kehret, Peg. *I'm Not Who You Think I Am*. Dutton Children's Books, 1999. ISBN 0-525-46153-1
    Two separate plots keep thirteen-year-old Ginger anxious and upset. First, Ginger is being stalked by a mentally ill woman who thinks Ginger is her long lost daughter. The second plot involves Ginger in a controversy at school when her favorite teacher, the girls' basketball coach Mr. Wren, is being harassed by a very influential parent, Mrs. Vaughn. Ginger is a resourceful teen who follows her conscience and does the right thing in this thriller that is filled with many moral dilemmas. (5–9)

Koss, Amy Golden. *The Ashwater Experiment*. Dial Books for Young Readers, 1999. ISBN 0-8037-2391-1
    Twelve-year-old Hilary has attended seventeen schools as her parents travel around the country selling their wares at craft fairs. But now they are going to stay in Ashwater, California. This means that Hilary will remain at a school for a whole year, and she sets out with enthusiasm to make some friends at her eighteenth school. She soon is included in the circle of friends of the most popular girl, and she makes friends with a very intelligent but klutzy girl who is a loner. But how will Hilary feel when her parents are on the move again? (5–8)

Naylor, Phyllis Reynolds. *Walker's Crossing*. Aladdin Paperbacks, 1999. ISBN 0-689-84261-9
    Ryan Walker is faced with tough moral choices when his older brother joins a militia group, the Mountain Patriot's Association. The association believes that the local lands are being stolen by immigrants, the federal government, and minorities, and they respond by training and raising arms. Loyalties are tested in Ryan's home and community when a plane is mistakenly shot down by Gil's brigade. (5–9)

Philbrick, Rodman. *The Last Book in the Universe*. Scholastic, 2000. ISBN 0-439-08658-9
    In a post-apocalyptic future, an epileptic teenager, Spaz, is told by gang members to rob an old man named Ryter. Instead, Spaz makes friends with him. When Spaz learns that his sister is dying, Ryter leads him on a dangerous journey to see his sister. (6–9)

Rinaldi, Ann. *Ameilia's War*. Scholastic, 1999. ISBN 0-590-11744-0
    During the Civil War, the town of Hagerstown, Maryland, is split in its loyalties, but Amelia is determined to take a neutral stance. When a confederate general threatens to burn down the town unless he receives ransom money, it is Amelia who outwits the general and saves the day. This story is based on an actual event. (6–8)

YA (grades 8–12)

Alvarez, Julia. *Before We Were Free.* Alfred A. Knopf, 2002. ISBN 0-375-81544-9

Twelve-year-old Anita lives on the compound with her grandparents, aunts, and uncles. Anita is confused and having a hard time adjusting to the fact that all of her extended family has left the Dominican Republic for the United States. Initially, she is unenlightened about the political situation, but her family begins to trust her as their freedoms are compromised. The secret police visit the compound and search the homes, while their uncle plots to overturn El Jefe, Truiillo. Anita's sister is spirited away to the United States because Truiillo has taken an interest in her. Anita wishes that they could all leave, but her family believes that they have a responsibility to try to change the dictatorship and that someday they will be free. Eventually Papa is taken away, and Anita and her mother spend two months in hiding until they are evacuated. (6–10).

Bennett, James W. *Blue Star Rapture.* Simon & Schuster, 1998. ISBN 0-689-81580-8

T. J. pretends to help the big guy, Tyrone and in doing so he feels important. College coaches know that T. J. looks out for Tyrone, and ask him to encourage Tyrone and keep track of any of his communications with other college scouts. After the two of them go to Full Court, a basketball camp, T. J. realizes that he, too, is a work in transition. In the future, he will be out of the loop with Tyrone. T. J. is a good player in his own way and needs to perfect himself. (7–12, mature language)

Blackwood, Gary. *The Year of the Hangman.* Penguin Putnam Books, 2002. ISBN 0-525-46921-4

Creighton Brown is abducted and taken to a ship bound for the colonies. Creighton learns that it is his mother who is placing him in the custody of her brother, Colonel Gower. This book addresses the question, what if George Washington were in custody and the leaders of the American Revolution were expelled from the colonies? Creighton meets many of the leaders and is pulled between spying for his uncle and the British and his new found loyalty to the Americans and their cause for liberty and freedom. (8–10)

Chambers, Aiden. *Postcards from No Man's Land.* Penguin Putnam Books, 2002. ISBN 0-525-46863-3

Jacob Todd travels to Amsterdam, in place of his grandmother, to attend a ceremony honoring his grandfather and other soldiers who liberated Holland from Germany in World War II. Young Jacob meets the dying Geertrui who hid his injured grandfather, Jacob, and learns how he died before the war ended. Geertrui reveals a secret she has kept all these years. She had relations with Jacob and has a child from the relationship. Geertrui has lived this lie long enough and unburdens her soul to young Jacob in narratives revealing both the past and present. (9–up)

 There are no secrets to success: don't waste time looking for them. Success is the result of perfection, hard work, learning from failure, loyalty to those for whom you work, and persistence.
—Colin Powell

Koontz, Dean. *Odd Thomas.* Bantam Books, 2003. ISBN 0-553-80249-8

Odd Thomas, short-order cook at the town grill, is able to communicate with the dead. They come to him with unresolved issues. Odd is also able to see "bodachs" or evil beings, and they arrive in great numbers, along with a stranger, to the town. Odd is sure that something awful is going to happen, and he works at a fast pace to try to set things right. (General Adult)

Randle, Kristen D. *Breaking Rank*. HarperCollins, 2002. ISBN 0-380-73281-5

Baby spends most of his life as a member of a group called the Clan. The members of the Clan wear black and are generally feared and scorned by classmates and neighbors. Baby goes against the group when he takes honor classes in high school. He is assigned a peer tutor, a pretty, well-liked girl named Casey. Casey helps Baby get into the mainstream at school, but this threatens the Clan and the Cribs, the popular kids who wear letter jackets. Soon, the inevitable happens, and choices have to be made. (9–up)

Shusterman, Neal. *The Shadow Club Rising*. Dutton Children's Books, 2002. ISBN 0-5254-6835-8

New kid, Alex Smartz, is very talented and makes the rest of the kids feel inferior. When he becomes the victim of a number of pranks, most of the students think the culprit is Jared, the former leader of the Shadow Club. In the previous book, members of the Shadow Club pulled pranks that became deadly. To flush out the real culprit, Jared turns bad again. (7–10)

Temple, Frances. *The Beduins' Gazelle*. Orchard, 1996. ISBN 0-531-08869-3

The year is 1302, and Halima is pledged to Atiyah when they are children. Atiyah is sent away to the city and Halima becomes lost in a sandstorm; she is found near death by a huntsman from an enemy. The sheikh tells Halima that she must accept the will of Allah and become his youngest wife. Atiyah learns that Halima is missing and with a friend locates the enemy tribe. The young men are in grave danger, for if the sheikh knows they are in the guest tent, they will be killed, and the sheikh will keep Halima for himself. (7–up)

Yep, Laurence. *Dragon's Gate*. HarperCollins, 1993. ISBN 0-06-440489-7

Otter is forced to leave China when he accidentally kills a Manchu soldier. He flees to the Golden Mountain to follow his father and uncle who are coolies working on the transcontinental railroad. (7–up)

Yolen, Jane. *Armageddon Summer*. Harcourt Children's Books, 1998. ISBN 0-15-201767-4

Their parents drag Marina and Jed to the mountain retreat of Reverend Beelson to wait for Armageddon—July 27, 2000. (7–up)

Nonfiction

Fritz, Jean. *Leonardo's Horse*. G. P. Putnam's Sons, 2001. ISBN 0-399-23576-0

This book begins with a brief biography of Leonardo da Vinci and describes his desire to make a bronze horse for the duke of Milan. In November 1493, Leonardo makes a clay model of the horse, but he never completes the project. In 1988, Charles Dent, demonstrating loyalty to the project, works to complete the bronze horse that Leonardo never finished, with hopes of giving the horse to Italy one day as a present from the American people. (3–6)

Kuklin, Susan. *Iqbal Masih and the Crusaders against Child Slavery*. Henry Holt, 1998. ISBN 0-8050-5459-6

Iqbal Masih was sold into slavery to work in the carpet industry at age four and freed at age ten. After speaking about his working conditions in Pakistan, Europe, and the United States, he went back to Pakistan and was murdered at age twelve. The final section discusses what schools are doing to organize boycotts and protests about this tragic problem. (7–up)

Stanley, Diane. *Saladin: Noble Prince of Islam*. HarperCollins, 2002. ISBN 0688171354

Just before he died in 1193, Saladin gave his eldest son advice on being a king: "win the hearts of your people and watch over their prosperity; for it is to secure their happiness that you are appointed by God and by me." Saladin was a gentle Muslim warrior who shocked his enemy with his mercy when victorious. He was a warrior who longed for peace and was considered a "marvel of his time." (3–7)

Venezia, Mike. *Johann Sebastian Bach.* Children's Press, 1998. ISBN 0-516-20760-1

The father of seventeen children, Johann Bach was busy taking care of his family. He became director of music in Leipzig, Germany, and was "responsible for composing and directing music for four churches, a school choir, a university choir, and any music the city might need for special events." Later, baroque music would go out of favor, but Bach was loyal to the style even though he was criticized for this loyalty. (3–6)

Chapter 8

Honesty

Related Virtues

Integrity, diligence, fortitude, fairness, sincerity, and truthfulness

Definition

The quality or condition of being honest; integrity, truthfulness, sincerity

Honesty in Action

- ✧ Tell the truth.
- ✧ Don't deceive others.
- ✧ Don't cheat.
- ✧ Set a good example for others.
- ✧ Be fair when you participate in sports.
- ✧ Be fair to classmates.
- ✧ Don't share your work with others.
- ✧ Don't cut and paste work off the Internet.
- ✧ Don't plagiarize.
- ✧ Even if it is uncomfortable, tell the truth!

People Who Have Demonstrated This Virtue

- ✧ Confucius
- ✧ Barbara Jordan
- ✧ Cochise

♦ Martin Luther

♦ Ruth Bader Ginsburg

♦ Eleanor Roosevelt

♦ Karen Silkwood

♦ Betty Ford

♦ George Washington

♦ Miguel de Cervantes

Discussion Questions

♦ Have you ever been rewarded for doing something honest?

♦ Is honesty always rewarded by others?

♦ What are lies?

♦ Are there degrees of lies?

♦ Are there people whom you do not trust because they have lied to you?

♦ Why do people tell lies?

♦ Are there good lies?

♦ What does the Golden Rule say about honesty?

♦ What are some situations in which it is difficult to be honest?

♦ Why do people cheat?

♦ Which character in the book you read demonstrated the virtue of honesty?

♦ How did he or she demonstrate this virtue?

♦ What were the consequences of not being honest?

♦ How would the story have turned out differently if the main character had not made the choices she or he did?

♦ How would you define honesty using the events in this story?

Related Topics to Explore

♦ Tall tales—read classic examples, determine what they are, write some

♦ Truth in advertising—how important is it? What is propaganda? As a society, how much do we value truth in advertising?

♦ Magicians—based on deception; the hand is quicker than the eye

♦ Truth serum—what is it, how is it used?

♦ Famous lies—explore stories such as "Pinocchio"

♦ Whistle-blowers

♦ The whole truth and nothing but the truth—history and use of this oath

♦ Cheating and plagiarism—challenge for today's young people

♦ Famous poems about honesty

♦ Honesty in advertising

Annotated Titles

Picture Books

Aylesworth, Jim. *Old Black Fly.* Henry Holt, 1995. ISBN 0-8050-3925-2
Old black fly gets into trouble twenty-six ways to match the number of letters in the alphabet
—from stealing some jelly to snoozing on Gramma's quilt until—swat!! (ps–3)

Bunting, Eve. *A Day's Work.* Clarion Books, 1994. ISBN 0-395-84518-1
Francisco helps his non-English-speaking grandfather get a gardening job by saying in English that they are gardeners. Their deception is exposed when they make errors on the job, and the grandfather refuses to accept their pay until they fix their errors. In this way, he teaches Francisco an important lesson and is able to keep his job with his new employer. (00-3)

Ernst, Lisa Campbell. *When Bluebell Sang.* Simon & Schuster, 1989. ISBN 0-02-733561-5
Bluebell is a singing cow who travels all around the country giving concerts. Big Eddie, her talent agent, is happily making money, but Bluebell is missing the green pastures of home. Bluebell plans her escape and leaves all the fame and fortune behind. (ps–1)

Falconer, Ian. *Olivia Saves the Circus.* Atheneum Children's Books, 2001. ISBN 0-689-82954-X
Olivia tells her classmates about her vacation and trip to the circus and explains that all the circus performers were sick. Olivia takes over and becomes the tattooed lady, lion tamer, tightrope walker, and clown. According to Olivia, she saved the circus, but then her teacher asks if what she says is true. Olivia responds, "Pretty all true." (ps–2)

Gill-Brown, Vanessa. *Rufferella.* Scholastic, 2000. ISBN 0-439-25617-8
Diamante's favorite fairy tale is Cinderella, and one day, she decides to turn her dog into a girl. Ruff becomes Ruff-erella. Rufferella is famous and is invited to the ball at the palace. Rufferella has one weakness: sausages. When they are served sausages at the long dinner table at the ball, Rufferella reverts back to Ruff and jumps up on the table. Later the queen sends a note of advice to Rufferella: "One is often best off if one allows one to be oneself." (ps–1)

Keller, Holly. *That's Mine, Horace.* Greenwillow Books, 2000. ISBN 0-688-17159-1
Horace finds an orange truck on the playground, and he takes it. Walter tells Horace that the truck is his. Horace lies to the teacher and says it is his. Horace pretends to be sick and stays home the next day. The kids send get-well cards including a note from Walter that says he can keep the truck until he feels better. When Horace comes back to school, he returns the truck to Walter. (ps–2)

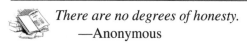

There are no degrees of honesty.
—Anonymous

McKissack, Patricia C. *The Honest-to-Goodness Truth.* Atheneum Children's Books, 2000. ISBN 0-689-82668-0
Libby learns that she must always tell the truth, and she sets out to do just that. But after a day of being very truthful to everyone, she finds that she has upset a lot of people. She examines what she has said and goes back to each person and apologizes. She learns that there are more appropriate ways to tell the truth! (ps–3)

Meddaugh, Susan. *Martha Blah Blah.* Houghton Mifflin, 1996. ISBN 0-395-79755-1

Martha is a dog who is able to talk because she eats vegetable soup with all the letters of the alphabet. One day she tries to speak and finds that she can only say, "Blah, blah." She starts an investigation and discovers that the soup company is leaving out letters to save money. Martha encourages them to tell the truth and include all the letters! (ps–3)

Ness, Evaline. *Sam, Bangs & Moonshine.* Henry Holt, 1996. ISBN 0-8050-0314-2

Samantha has a habit of telling stories—her father calls it moonshine. Usually her stories are harmless, but one day her story puts her friend and her cat in grave danger. Sam learns an important lesson about telling the truth. (2–up)

Rohman, Eric. *Time Flies.* Random House, 1994. ISBN 0-517-59598-2

This natural history museum is not as it appears. A bird flies around the exhibit and encounters a dinosaur that briefly appears to come to life. This is a wordless book that tests your imagination. (00–3)

Shannon, Margaret. *Gullible's Troubles.* Houghton Mifflin, 1998. ISBN 0-395-83933-5

Gullible is a little guinea pig who believes everything his relatives tell him. (ps–3)

Primary (grades 1–3)

Brown, Marc. *Arthur's Computer Disaster.* Little, Brown and Company, 1997. ISBN 0-316-11016-7

When Arthur's mom has to go to the office, she tells Arthur not to touch the computer, but Arthur wants to finish a game he is playing. Arthur and Buster load the game, and at a crucial point they both reach for the mouse, and the computer goes blank. When Arthur's mom calls to ask how things are going, Arthur lies and says fine, but he is actually very worried. Arthur confesses to his mom when she gets home and learns that the computer is not broken, but she is disappointed that Arthur doesn't call when he is in trouble. (00–3)

Calmenson, Stephanie. *The Principal's New Clothes.* Scholastic, 1989. ISBN 0-590-41822-X

The principal is the sharpest dresser in town, and when two strangers come to town, they sell him a one-of-a-kind suit. This suit will allow the principal to tell whether someone is stupid or not good at his or her job if the suit appears to be invisible to that person. When the principal tries on the suit, he is surprised that it appears invisible to him. He wears the suit to school, and no one tells him that they only see him in his underwear until a kindergartener tells the truth. (ps–3)

 The person who is straightforward and honest doesn't have to worry about a faulty memory.
—Anonymous

Cohen, Miriam. *Liar, Liar, Pants on Fire!* Random House, 1987. ISBN 0-440-44755-0

Alex is the new boy at school, and when anyone says they have or can do something, Alex can do one better. Soon the children chant "liar, liar, pants on fire!" to him, but Alex merely wants to be noticed and make friends. Eventually he does. (00–2)

dePaola, Tomie. *Bonjour, Mister Satie.* G. P. Putnam's Sons, 1991. ISBN 0-399-21782-7

Mr. Satie comes to the United States to visit with his niece and nephew. He tells them about an incident with two artists in Paris, France. Pablo and Henri both arrive at the same time with their art to display, and they ask Mr. Satie which is the best. Mr. Satie is honest and declares that both are very good, but they are different. One cannot compare apples with oranges. Both taste good, but they are not the same. The artists remain friends, and Mr. Satie saves the day. (ps–3)

Goble, Paul. *Iktomi and the Boulder.* Orchard Books, 1988. ISBN 0-531-05911-1

Iktomi is a trickster, a liar, and mischief maker. He is on his way to visit relatives. When he becomes hot, he gives his blanket to the boulder, saying he feels sorry for it being so long in the sun. Later on when it looks like rain, Iktomi takes his blanket back saying he was only lending it to the boulder. After the rain, the boulder comes crashing down on him, and Iktomi cannot move. The animals try to help Iktomi, but it isn't until he makes up stories about the boulder that the bats strike it over and over until the boulder is nothing but chips. This story explains why bats have flat faces and why there are small rocks all over the Great Plains. (ps–2)

Krensky, Stephen. *Arthur and the Cootie-Catcher.* Little, Brown and Company, 1999. ISBN 0-316-11993-8

Rubella shows off her cootie-catcher at Prunella's half-birthday party. Rubella promises that her cootie-catcher will change their lives forever. When Arthur and his friends ask a question, Prunella works the cootie-catcher and then lifts a flap for the answer. Rubella warns that if they do not obey the cootie-catcher, then they will be cursed. Is the cootie-catcher able to foretell the future, or is it just a coincidence? Includes instructions on how to make your own cootie catcher. (0–3)

_____. *The Mystery of the Stolen Bike.* Little, Brown and Company, 1998. ISBN 0-316-11570-3

Francine wants a new bike. Her father gives her a new bike, which is actually the bike he rode when he was a kid. Francine is embarrassed about the rusted purple bike with an orange banana seat. She parks it behind the garbage cans, and when the garbage collectors pick it up and put it in their truck, Francine says the bike was stolen by a bike-eating truck. Francine is forced to tell the truth when her friends accuse Binky of stealing the bike. Francine and her father find the bike at the junkyard, and together they fix it up. (1–3)

Marshall, James. *Fox on the Job.* Dial Books for Young Readers, 1988. ISBN 0-8037-0350-3

Fox wrecks his bike, and he tries to earn some money for a new one but is fired from most of his jobs. Fox gets a job in a shoe store, and the owner asks him if he is honest. Fox replies that he is, but when a lady with big feet comes in, he is a little too honest and loses the job. (0–3)

McDonald, Megan. *The Potato Man.* Orchard, 1991. ISBN 0-531-05914-6

Grandpa tells his grandchildren a story about when he was a boy. The story is of the potato man who is a vegetable peddler with one eye. Young grandpa's luck starts to turn when he steals the potatoes that bounce off the peddler's wagon. His bad luck changes when he encounters the potato man's kindness one winter day. (ps–3)

O'Connor, Jane. *Nina, Nina Star Ballerina.* Grosset & Dunlap, 1997. ISBN 0-448-41611-5

Nina is in a show, and she is a star in a dance called the night sky. She tells her friend that she is a star, and her friend tells her other friends that she is the star in the dance. Nina is embarrassed and doesn't know what to say. When her friend Ann asks to come to the show, Nina limps around the house hoping to avoid dancing. Nina confesses to Ann and learns that it doesn't matter that Nina is not the star. (ps–1)

Park, Barbara. *Junie B. Jones and Some Sneaky Peeky Spying.* Random House Books for Young Readers, 1994. ISBN 0-679-95101-6

Junie B. Jones is in kindergarten and can't resist sneaking up on people and spying. When she spots her teacher in the grocery store, Junie follows her. Her teacher, Mrs., picks up some grapes and samples them without paying for them. Junie is shocked that her teacher isn't perfect because eating the grapes is the same as stealing. Will Mrs. explain herself? (1–3)

Wilhelm, Hans. *Tyrone the Double Dirty Rotten Cheater.* Scholastic, 1991. ISBN 0-590-44079-9
Tyrone the horrible, goes to Swamp Island for a week with friends. Tyrone is a bully and wins all the games by cheating. He is pleased with the way things are going until he tries to cheat one too many times. (1–3)

Intermediate (grades 3–5)

Banks, Lynne Reid. *The Indian in the Cupboard.* Morrow Avon, 1999. ISBN 0-380-60012-9
Omri's big brother gives him an old medicine cabinet for his birthday, and when Omri puts a plastic toy Indian in the cabinet before going to sleep, the magic begins. The Indian and all subsequent toys placed in the cabinet become real and want to be part of Omri's life. (4–7)

 When in doubt, tell the truth.
—Mark Twain

Bauer, Marion Dane. *On My Honor.* Houghton Mifflin, 1986. ISBN 0-89919-439-7
Joel and Tony are on a bicycle trip to a state park when Joel dares Tony to race him across the Vermillion River to the sandbar. The boys know that the river is dangerous, but they both jump in. Joel gets to the sandbar, but Tony does not. Joel is terrified of letting his parents know of his disobedience and overwhelmed by guilt in the drowning death of his friend. (4–7)

Christopher, Matt. *Undercover Tailback.* Little, Brown and Company, 1992. ISBN 0-316-14251-4
Parker has a long history of telling lies, so when he tries to report a suspicious person in the coach's office, no one believes him. Parker has a lot to do to set things straight and regain his credibility. (3–6)

Lowry, Lois. *Your Move, J. P.!* Dell Yearling Books, 1991. ISBN 0-440-40497-5
J. P. is a bright boy who is an excellent chess player. A new student, Angela, arrives and quickly steals his heart. J. P. tries very hard to impress her and finds himself telling some fibs. (3–7)

Naylor, Phyllis Reynolds. *Shiloh.* Atheneum Children's Books, 1991. ISBN 0-689-31614-3
Eleven-year-old Marty lives with his poor family in the mountains of West Virginia. His neighbor, Judd, mistreats his dog, and Marty hides the dog to keep it safe. Marty's lies, omissions, and blackmail force a deal with Judd. Marty works for Judd to pay him for the dog, which Judd says he can keep. Marty's parents hear a different story from their son. (4–6)

Middle School (grades 5–8)

Avi. *Midnight Magic.* Scholastic, 1999. ISBN 0-590-36035-3
Fabrizio is the servant and assistant to Mangus, a magician, in the 1400s. Mangus is under house arrest, and his life is spared after he repents of being a magician. So why is the king summoning Fabrizio and Mangus to the castle to solve a mystery? Mangus has given up creating the illusion of magic and wants only to speak the truth, but many lives are at stake—including his own. (5–9)

———. *Never Mind.* HarperCollins, 2004. ISBN 0-06-054315-9
Told in alternating chapters, the twins, Meg and Edward, give their versions of one week in their school lives. They both attend different schools, and Meg is trying to become part of the High Achievers Clubs. This starts a series of lies that involves her twin brother, and they quickly put together a band called "Never Mind." They are scheduled to play at a Saturday party of one

of the most popular girls in Meg's school, who thinks Meg's twin is her boyfriend even though she has never met him. (5–up)

_____. *The True Confessions of Charlotte Doyle.* Holt, Rinehart & Winston, 1999. ISBN 0-03-054709-1

Thirteen-year-old Charlotte Doyle is the only passenger and the only female on the Seahawk. The rat-infested ship has a mutinous crew and a ruthless captain. During the dangerous journey on the high seas, Charlotte is charged with murder and sentenced to hang! (5–7)

Choldenko, Gennifer. *Notes from a Liar and Her Dog.* Penguin Putnam, 2001. ISBN 0-399-23591-4

Antonia McPherson is an experienced liar. Her mother always thinks she is wrong, her older sister makes fun of her best friend, and her younger sister is always tattling on her. Ant is devoted to her Chihuahua, Pistachio, and to her best friend, Harrison. A teacher finally sees the reason for Ant's lies, and her involvement brings about a confrontation between Ant and her mother. (5–9)

Coville, Bruce. *The Skull of Truth: A Magic Shop Book.* Harcourt Children's Books, 1997. ISBN 0-15-275457-1

Charlie, who has a history of lying, has become the target of bullies. He is against a plan to drain a local swamp and build an industrial park. He suddenly finds the skull of truth that prevents him from telling any lies, and thus he gets into even more trouble. (3–7)

DeClements, Barthe. *Liar, Liar.* Marshall Cavendish, 1998. ISBN 0-7614-5021-1

Gretchen Griswald lives with her dad, and her two brothers and one stepbrother live with her mom. She has a good friend named Susan November and gets along well at school until a new girl, Marybelle, moves into town. Marybelle starts telling tales about the teacher and classmates. Soon the girls she likes most are snubbing Gretchen. Her brother helps her get to the bottom of the problem. (3–7)

 The very spring and root of honesty and virtue lie in good education.
—Plutarch

Holub, Joseph. *The Robber and Me.* Henry Holt, 1997. ISBN 0-8050-5599-1

Boniface Schroll, a young orphan, is delivered to his uncle, the mayor of Graab, a remote village in Germany. The driver abandons Boniface in the middle of the forest with instructions on how to find the village. Boniface is rescued by a strange man who wears a tall black hat. Could he be the Robber Knapp? The townspeople blame Robber Knapp for a number of holdups that have taken place, and his children are treated badly. Boniface knows that the Robber Knapp is not the thief, but he doesn't want to jeopardize his struggling relationship with his uncle and thus lose his new home. Will Boniface risk all and tell the truth about Robber Knapp? (3–7)

Smith, Roland. *Zach's Lie.* Hyperion, 2001. ISBN 0-440-40865-2

Jack Osborne, his mother, and sister enter the witness protection program after they are threatened by drug dealers. Jack becomes Zach Granger, and they begin a new life in a small town. Zach knows that their lives may have been spared but feels that reality is "lives" missing the letter V. (5–9)

White, Ruth. *Belle Prater's Boy.* Farrar, Straus & Giroux, 1996. ISBN 0-374-30668-0

When Belle Prater disappears, her boy Woodrow comes to live with his grandparents in Coal Station, Virginia. Woodrow's cousin, Gypsy, lives next door and tries to find out about his mother's disappearance. She has secrets of her own and wonders how Woodrow can adjust to his mother's disappearance when she can't understand her father's death. Woodrow eventually shares the real story of his mother. (5–9)

YA (grades 8–12)

Avi. *Nothing But the Truth.* Avon Books, 1991. ISBN 0-380-71907-X

Phillip is looking for a way to get transferred out of Mrs. Narwins's homeroom and English class. Phillip does not fulfill the requirements of his English class, so he receives a D, which means that he cannot be on the track team. Phillip convinces himself that Mrs. Narwin does not like him. After the morning announcements, students are asked to rise and stand at respectful, silent attention during the playing of the national anthem. Phillip begins humming and continues in spite of Mrs. Narwin's request for silence. Phillip insists that he is not disrespectful when he is "singing" the national anthem and that he wants to be transferred out of her homeroom and English class. How far is Phillip willing to press this issue? (6–10)

A lie has speed, but truth has endurance.
—Edgar J. Mohn

Cappo, Nan Willard. *Cheating Lessons.* Simon Pulse, 2003. ISBN 0-439-28603-4

Bernadette is the star of Wickham High's debate team, and she scores first place in a written test that allows the school to compete in the much coveted Classics Bowl State Championship. This will pit Wickham, a public school, against Pinehurst, a prestigious private school. But as the team prepares for the event, Bernadette becomes suspicious of their English teacher and coach, Mr. Malory. She feels that her teammates are not prepared and that the teacher changed some of their answers so that they could be in the contest. She discovers that Mr. Malory is dating one of the judges of the Classics Bowl. Bernadette has to make a serious decision because a lot is at stake—recognition for her school and a $10,000 college scholarship for each winning team member. (7–up)

Cooney, Caroline B. *The Face on the Milk Carton.* Dell, 1991. ISBN 0-440-22065-3

Janie Johnson recognizes a photo of herself on a milk carton—a missing three-year-old girl, kidnapped from a New Jersey shopping mall. This happened twelve years ago. Janie has to face the very real possibility that the Johnsons are not her real parents and try to find out the truth. (7–12)

Cormier, Robert. *The Chocolate War.* Pantheon Books, 1974. ISBN 0-394-82805-4

Jerry has a poster of a solitary man standing on the beach, mounted inside his locker. Inscribed on the poster is the slogan, "Do I dare disturb the universe?" Jerry defies a teacher and Archie, the leader of the Vigils, an underground organization, when he refuses to sell chocolates as part of a school fund-raiser. He sadly learns that people only let you do your own thing when it happens to be their own thing as well. (6–up)

Greene, Bette. *Summer of My German Soldier.* Penguin Group, 2003. ISBN 0-8037-2869-7

German prisoners are brought to a camp in a small Arkansas town during World War II. Patty, who is twelve years old and Jewish, makes friends with one of the prisoners, Anton, who has escaped. She helps him and grows to love him. Patty is rejected by both parents and has a brutal life at home, so her special relationship with Anton is very important to her. She is eager to give everything up for the love of this prison escapee. (6–12)

Griffin, Adele. *Amandine.* Hyperion Books, 2001. ISBN 0-7868-0618-4

Ninth-grader Delia moves from New York mid–school year. She is overweight, shy, and feels like she never does anything right in her parent's eyes. Delia meets Amandine, part artist, part ballet dancer, part actress. Amandine plays dangerous games; she senses Delia's loneliness and manipulates her. Delia tells Amandine lies that will come back to haunt her. Amandine also tells lies, and when Delia has enough courage to break Amandine's hold over her, Amandine seeks revenge by telling a serious lie about Delia's father. (6–9)

Hautman, Pete. *Godless*. Simon Pulse, 2004. ISBN 0-689-86278-4

Jason Bock questions the religion of his parents and on a whim forms a new religion, the Church of the Ten-Legged God, formerly known as a water tower. Jason's best friend, Shin, is the First Keeper of the Sacred Text, and he writes as if the water tower is channeling through him. Henry, who is a bully without limits, is named the High Priest because he is the one who can show them the way up the water tower. When Henry slips over the edge of the water tower, the religion begins to dissolve until Jason is the only remaining member. (7–up)

Naidoo, Beverley. *The Other Side of Truth*. HarperCollins, 2001. ISBN 0-06-029628-3

Sade and Femi witness their mother's death in Nigeria. Their father, a reporter, has been threatened because of his outspoken opinions. Sade and Femi are smuggled illegally to London and encounter many frightening experiences when the uncle they are supposed to stay with mysteriously disappears. (6–up)

Nolan, Peggy. *The Spy Who Came in from the Sea*. Pineapple Press, 1999. ISBN 1-56164-186-3

During World War II, Francis moves to Jacksonville, Florida, to be near his dad, but in the meantime, unbeknownst to Frank and his mother, Francis's father is shipped out on an aircraft carrier. Frank's mom gets a job in the shipbuilding yard, and they rent a "chicken coop" just off the beach. At his new school, Franks becomes known as an exaggerator. One evening, Frank observes a submarine momentarily stuck on a sandbar and a raft with a man climbing out of it into the surf. The man staggers up the beach and buries a chest in the sand before he makes his way to the main road. Frank is sure he just witnessed a spy being dropped off on the beach, but how will he convince others that this time he is not "crying wolf"? (5–9)

 Flattery makes friends, truth enemies.
—Spanish Proverb

Oates, Joyce Carol. *Big Mouth & Ugly Girl*. HarperCollins, 2002. ISBN 0-06-623758-0

"Big Mouth" Matt Donaghy is suspended from school when someone tells that he has threatened to blow up the school. Ursula Riggs, who calls herself, Ugly Girl, hears what Matt says and comes to his defense despite warnings from her mother. Matt is shut out by his former friends and begins an awkward friendship with Ugly Girl. When Matt's family decides to sue the school and his accusers, things almost get out of hand. (8–up)

Sachar, Louis. *Holes*. Farrar, Straus & Giroux, 1998. ISBN 0-374-33265-7

Stanley Yelnats IV's great-grandfather lost his entire fortune, and a curse was placed on his descendants. Stanley continues to have the same kind of bad luck. He is sent to Camp Green Lake for a crime he didn't commit. Camp Green Lake is not at all what its name suggests. It is desolate and barren with no water in sight, so fences and guards are unnecessary. His punishment is to dig a hole five feet by five feet in width and depth every day in the hot sun before he is allowed to do anything else. Every thing changes when Stanley finds a small gold tube with the initials of KB. (7–12)

Salisbury, Graham. *Lord of the Deep*. Bantam Doubleday Dell, 2001. ISBN 0-385-72918-9

Thirteen-year-old Mikey Donovan is delighted when his stepfather, Bill, asks him to help out with his boat, the *Crystal-C* and his charter fishing business in the Hawaiian Islands. Mikey calls Bill the "Lord of the Deep" because he is an excellent deep-sea fisherman. He is also kind to his mother and little brother, who is blind. Two tourists hire on the boat, and Mikey helps one of them capture a record-breaking mahi-mahi. Mikey's faith in Bill is shaken when the tourist makes a dishonest offer and Bill accepts. (5–up)

Nonfiction

Adler, David A. *A Picture Book of Abraham Lincoln.* Holiday House, 1990. ISBN 0-8234-0731-4
  This is a brief narrative about "Honest Abe"—Abraham Lincoln—from his birth on February 12, 1809, to his assassination by John Wilkes Booth. (1–3)

 I have not observed men's honesty to increase with their riches.
    —Thomas Jefferson

Kundhardt, Edith. *Honest Abe.* Greenwillow Books, 1993. ISBN 0-688-11189-0
  This is a brief biography of Abraham Lincoln, called "Abe" or "Honest Abe." "Once a woman paid him six and a quarter cents too much. He walked three miles to find her and pay her back." (K–3)

Truth & Lies: An Anthology of Poems. Edited by Patrice Vecchione. Henry Holt, 2001. ISBN 0-8050-6479-6
  "Lies can be used to hurt, manipulate, or to protect…. Poetry is a particular way of telling the truth." Read, feel, and absorb the poems about truth and lies from different time periods and cultures. (7–10)

Chapter 9

Cooperation

Related Virtues

Peacemaking, harmony, compromise, working together, sharing, uniting, community building, and tranquility

Definition

Joint operation or action, to work or act together toward a common end or purpose

Cooperation in Action

- ✧ Work together for the good of your school community.
- ✧ Support your school's activities.
- ✧ Work well with others in groups and teams.
- ✧ Be supportive of the efforts of your classmates.
- ✧ Be a leader in your school community.
- ✧ Do not argue.
- ✧ Be a peacemaker whenever you have the opportunity.
- ✧ Try to find a compromise in every difficult situation.

People Who Have Demonstrated This Virtue

- ✧ Jimmy Carter
- ✧ Colin Powell
- ✧ Wright Brothers
- ✧ Dag Hammarskjold
- ✧ Margaret Mead

Organizations

♦ United Nations

Discussion Questions

♦ How do you cooperate with your family?

♦ What do you like best about competition?

♦ What do you like best about cooperation?

♦ Do you think that the future of the world depends on how well we cooperate with one another?

♦ Why is it sometimes difficult to be a peacemaker?

♦ Do you like to work in groups? Why or why not?

♦ Why is it sometimes difficult to share?

Related Topics to Explore

♦ Conflict resolution

♦ Bullies

♦ I-messages

♦ Historical conflicts resolved by cooperation

♦ Peace pipe

♦ Mediation and arbitration

Annotated Titles

Picture Books

Auch, Mary Jane. *Hen Lake*. Holiday House, 1995. ISBN 0-8234-1270-9
    Percival, the peacock, boasts that he can sing and dance better than any of the hens in the barnyard. Poulette challenges him to a talent contest and then pleads with four of her friends to join her in a ballet, Hen Lake. The hens cooperate, rise to the occasion, and outperform Percival. (ps–3)

Axelrod, Amy. *Pigs in the Pantry: Fun with Math and Cooking*. Simon & Schuster, 1997. ISBN 0-689-80665-5
    When Mrs. Pig was not feeling well, Mr. Pig and his piglets decide to fix her favorite dish, chili. Together they make the chili, as the dishes and mess in the kitchen grows and grows. Mrs. Pig feels much better when she wakes up—until she smells the smoke and takes one look at her kitchen. (0–4)

Cooper, Helen. *Pumpkin Soup*. Farrar, Straus & Giroux, 2005. ISBN 0-374-46031-0
    A cat, a squirrel, and a duck live together in a cabin deep in the woods. They cooperate to make pumpkin soup. All is peaceful until one day the duck decides he wants to be head cook. The three friends end up squabbling, and duck packs his things and leaves. When he doesn't come back, squirrel and cat try to make pumpkin soup, but it doesn't taste the same. They go out and look for duck, but to their surprise, duck is home waiting for them. Even though it is late,

they agree to make pumpkin soup, and they let duck do whatever he wants. Once again, the three friends are at peace. (ps–3)

Cronin, Doreen. *Click, Clack, Moo: Cows That Type.* Simon & Schuster, 2000. ISBN 0-689-83213-3

When Farmer Brown first hears his cows typing, he doesn't know what to make of it. The next morning, he receives a typed note requesting electric blankets because the cows are cold in the barn. When Farmer Brown refuses, the cows go on strike. Next the hens go on strike because they want electric blankets, too. Duck negotiates a settlement, electric blankets for the typewriter. Farmer Brown thinks that is a good deal. Duck will personally deliver the typewriter. But wait! The next morning Farmer Brown receives another typed note, and this time it is from Duck! (ps–3)

Isadora, Rachel. *Lili Backstage.* G. P. Putnam's Sons, 1997. ISBN 0-399-23025-4

Young Lili explores all the areas backstage in search of her grandfather, who plays the French horn in the orchestra pit. In doing so, she is reminded of all the things that must come together to put on a performance. (ps–3)

Keller, Holly. *Cecil's Garden.* Greenwillow Books, 2002. ISBN 0-06-029593-7

Cecil planned to help Posey and Jake plant a garden, but instead they spend the day arguing about what should be planted where. Cecil goes to visit his mice and mole friends and learns about cooperation after listening to them argue. (0–3)

Lionni, Leo. *Swimmy.* Alfred A. Knopf, 1968. ISBN 0-394-82620-5

This classic tale is about a school of red fish that is eaten by a larger fish; the surviving black fish is named Swimmy. Swimmy is very sad and lonely until he sees a school of little fish just like his own. The little red fish are afraid to play until Swimmy encourages them to swim together like the largest fish in the sea, and he will become the eye. (ps–3)

Munch, Robert. *We Share Everything.* Scholastic, 1999. ISBN 0-590-89600-8

A boy and a girl attend their first day of school. They walk into the kindergarten classroom and argue over the books and toys. The teacher says, "We share everything." So the boys and girls decide to share everything beginning with their shoes, shirts, and pants. Soon the whole class is sharing, too! (ps–1)

Ryan, Pam Muñoz. *Mice and Beans.* Scholastic, 2001. ISBN 0-439-18303-0

Rosa Maria is preparing a big meal to celebrate her youngest grandchild's seventh birthday. She keeps setting mouse traps all week and thinks she is getting forgetful when they keep disappearing along with other items. Rosa Maria realizes that she forgot to fill the piñata with candy, but when the piñata breaks, candy falls to the ground. She wonders if she really has forgotten or if the mice worked together to help her. When she finds the telltale signs of mice in her house, she decides to let them be and never sets a mousetrap again. (ps–2)

 Great discoveries and improvements invariably involve the cooperation of many minds.
—Alexander Graham Bell

Primary (grades 1–3)

Deedy, Carmen Agra. *The Yellow Star: The Legend of King Christian X of Denmark.* Peachtree, 2000. ISBN 1-56145-208-4

The Danes are united in their love of King Christian X. When the Nazis invade Denmark, they state that all Jews must sew a visible yellow star on their clothing. The next morning the king rides through Copenhagen dressed with a yellow star visible on his clothing. The people of Denmark cooperate with the king, and soon everyone is wearing a yellow star. This traditional legend is a myth. (2–4)

Krensky, Stephen. *Francine, Believe It or Not.* Little, Brown and Company, 1999. ISBN 0-316-10463-9
    Muffy challenges Francine to be nice for one whole week, and if she is able to do so, then Muffy will give Francine her Princess Peach watch. Everyone is wondering what's the matter with Francine. They are not used to her being so cooperative and sharing. Will she be able to last the week without losing her temper? (K–3)

Lasky, Kathryn. *Marven of the Great North Woods.* Harcourt Brace, 1997. ISBN 0-15-216826-5
    This story is based on a true story about the author's father. Ten-year-old Marven is sent to a logging camp in the north woods after an outbreak of the influenza in Duluth, Minnesota. Marven travels alone on the train and skis to the edge of the forest and logging camp. Marven keeps the books and checks the bunkhouse at the third bell and wakes any remaining lumberjacks. Marven develops a relationship with all of the men, but especially with Jean Louis, who he mistakes for a grizzly bear. Marven awakens Jean Louis, and together they go to breakfast; Jean Louis eats whatever Marven could not or would not eat because he is Jewish. When the winter is over, Jean Louis accompanies Marven and partially carries him back to the tracks to meet the train to Duluth. (1–3)

McPhail, David. *Piggy's Pancake Parlor.* Dutton Children's Books, 2002. ISBN 0-525-45930-8
    Piggy, the runt of the litter, is cared for by Mr. and Mrs. Farmer Todd. Piggy is so good in the kitchen that Mrs. Farmer Todd teaches him how to make her delicious pancakes. Piggy meets Fox, also the runt of the litter, stealing eggs from the henhouse. Eventually, the two restore a vacant building and open a very successful pancake restaurant. (1–3)

Park, Barbara. *Junie B., First Grader: Boss of Lunch.* Random House, 2002. ISBN 0-375-81517-1
    Junie B. is in first grade and in trouble again because she just can't leave her new lunchbox alone during class. She meets her favorite cafeteria worker, Mrs. Gutzman, and she offers to let Junie help her in the cafeteria if Junie promises to follow the rules. (1–3)

Intermediate (grades 3–5)

Clements, Andrew. *Jake Drake Know-It-All.* Simon & Schuster, 2001. ISBN 0-689-83918-9
    Jake enters the third-grade science fair contest hoping to win the first-place prize, a top-of-the-line computer. Jake is focused on winning the prize and chooses to work alone and in secret. When his best friend decides to drop out of the contest, Jake asks Willie to join up with him. Together they learn, have fun, and work together on their project. They do not win first place, but Jake learns that he does not want to be a know-it-all. (2–5)

_____. *A Week in the Woods.* Simon & Schuster, 2002 ISBN 0-689-82596-X
    Mark is a new student in a small public school. He knows he will be going to a boarding school, so in the meantime he keeps his distance from the other students. When Mr. Maxwell announces the environmental camping trip, Mark comes around and signs up for the trip. On the first day of the trip, Mr. Maxwell finds that Mark has a tool that contains a knife, which is not allowed. He punishes Mark by attempting to send him home, but Mark runs away before that happens. Mr. Maxwell wants to teach Mark a lesson and follows him with the hope that he can rescue Mark. It turns out that Mr. Maxwell sprains his ankle; Mark is a prepared camper and rescues Mr. Maxwell. Together they make it back to camp. (4–6)

King-Smith, Dick. *Mr. Potter's Pet.* Hyperion, 1996. ISBN 0-7868-0174-3
> Everest, a rude, bossy mynah bird, brings together his master, Mr. Potter, and Margaret, the housekeeper, only to regret his matchmaking. (2–5)

Lee, Jeanne. *Bitter Dumplings.* Farrar, Straus & Giroux, 2002. ISBN 0-374-39966-2
> An old Chinese woman and a young girl, Mei Mei, both shunned by their betrotheds' families, team up and create a life for themselves making bitter dumplings and taking them to the market. One day the young girl encounters the emperor's treasure fleet. The hungry sailors and the captured ship's carpenter row ashore and greedily eat Mei Mei's bitter dumplings. The carpenter remembers the taste, follows Mei Mei, and realizes that he has found his village. He hides from the sailors, and the old woman reveals her dowry trunk, which she gladly gives to Mei Mei and the young man. "It was the beginning of a happy new life for them all." (2–5)

 We must be willing to learn the lesson that cooperation may imply compromise, but if it brings a world advance it is a gain for each individual nation.
—Eleanor Roosevelt

Morgenstern, Susie. *A Book of Coupons.* Viking, 2001. ISBN 0-670-89970-4
> It is the first day of school, and the kids are expecting a young teacher this year. Instead, an old, fat, wrinkly man, Monsieur Noel, is in class, and the first thing he does is hand each student a book of coupons. These coupons are unique—they say things such as "sleep late one day," "forget your homework," or "skip a day of school." Monsieur Noel gets into trouble with Incarnation Perez, the principal, for his undisciplined ways. Eventually Incarnation Perez has her way and Monsieur Noel's contract is not renewed. At the end-of-the-year party, Monsieur Noel admires those who have used their coupons and relates it to the fact that when you are born you have a whole book of coupons to use. In the end, the children give him a coupon for a well-deserved retirement. (3–6)

O'Brien, Robert. *Mrs. Frisby and the Rats of NIMH.* Atheneum Children's Books, 1974. ISBN 0-689-20651-8
> Mrs. Frisby must care for her four little children. One is sick with pneumonia, and Mrs. Frisby is greatly distressed because it is the time of the year when she must move her family to their summer living quarters. She seeks help from her friends, the rats from NIMH, who are amazingly intelligent having spent much of their lives in a laboratory. (4–7)

Wallace, Rich. *Technical Foul.* Viking, 2004. ISBN 0-14-240444-6
> Jared is the go-to guy on his basketball team, but he never learns when to pass the ball. Jared is thrown out of the game because of his temper. The rest of the team pulls together for the first win of the season. Jared and Spencer are the team leaders, but lately they are not getting along because of Jared's attitude. Will the boys overcome their differences, and will Jared quit trying to be a hero? (3–5)

Middle School (grades 5–8)

Bernardo, Anilu. *Jumping Off to Freedom.* Piñata Books, 1996. ISBN 1-55885-087-2
> Tired of living in fear in Cuba, David's father, Miguel, decides to build a raft and flee to Florida with his son and a friend. The journey is perilous and fraught with problems, but the group shows amazing determination, and by working together they somehow arrive safely in Florida. (6–12)

Cooney, Caroline B. *Flight Number 116 Is Down.* Scholastic Trade, 1992. ISBN 0-590-44465-4
A 747 crashes in deep woods behind Heidi's home, and she becomes involved in the massive rescue effort. She finds inner strength she never knew she had. (7–9)

Haddix, Margaret Peterson. *Takeoffs and Landings.* Simon & Schuster, 2001. ISBN 0-689-83299-0
Fifteen-year-old Chuck and fourteen-year-old Lori Lawson go along with their mother on a tour. Mother is a motivational speaker, and her frequent absences have made her two older children resentful. During the two weeks, they share many feelings, including some serious discussion about their Dad's accidental death. In the end, they are all better off for their time spent together. (4–6)

Korman, Gordon. *The 6th Grade Nickname Game.* Hyperion, 1998. ISBN 0-7868-1335-0
Eleven-year-old best friends, Wiley and Jeff, love to give all their classmates nicknames. Their new teacher, Mr. Hughes, who was a football coach, is now Mr. Huge. Jeff and Wiley give a cool nickname to the "blandest kid in school" and spread it around, then watch his popularity soar. However, they are unable to find a suitable nickname for the new girl, Cassandra. Their nickname for their class, Dim Bulbs, has everyone thinking that they can't possibly do well on the state reading test. If that's the case, then Mr. Huge will surely lose his job. (3–7)

 We may all have come on different ships, but we're in the same boat now.
—Martin Luther King, Jr.

Oppel, Kenneth. *Silverwing.* Aladdin Paperbacks, 1997. ISBN 0-689-82558-7
This adventure story is about Shade, the runt of the Silverwing bat colony who desires to see the sun. Young Shade is separated from the colony during the winter migration and thus begins his epic journey to locate the colony once again. (3–7)

Taylor, Theodore. *The Cay.* Random House, 1987. ISBN 0-385-07906-0
After the Germans torpedo the freighter on which Phillip and his mother are traveling, Phillip finds himself dependent on Timothy, an old, black West Indian sailor. They are shipwrecked, and there is just the two of them. This is the story of their struggle for survival and of Phillip's efforts to adjust to his blindness and to understand the dignified, wise, and loving old man who is his companion. (5–up)

YA (grades 8–12)

Bauer, Joan. *Hope Was Here.* Putnam, 2000. ISBN 0-399-23142-0
Sixteen-year-old Hope moves a long distance to Wisconsin with her aunt. They are going to help run the Welcome Stairways Diner. Hope soon finds herself involved in politics as she works together with the diner's owner in his campaign for mayor of the small town. The owner of the diner, G. T., has leukemia and is running against the previously undefeated mayor. (7–12)

Crutcher, Chris. *Whale Talk.* Greenwillow Books, 2001. ISBN 0-688-18019-1
T. J. is part black, part white, and part Japanese; he is adopted and lives in a predominantly white environment. He is a talented athlete but does not participate because he doesn't identify with the jock culture. When his English teacher and coach asks T. J. to be the anchor of the newly formed swim team, T. J. agrees if he can choose his teammates. T. J. selects the misfits of the school and forms a swim team for a high school that does not have a pool. (7–up)

Dessen, Sarah. *Someone Like You.* Penguin Putnam Books for Young Readers, 2000. ISBN 0-14-130268-0

Halley and Scarlett have been friends since grade school, and they turn to each other for support in their junior year. Two months after her boyfriend is killed in a motorcycle accident, Scarlett discovers she is pregnant. At the same time, Halley is dating Macon, a boy her parents have forbidden her to see. They must continue to cooperate and help each other through these hard times. (7–up, for mature readers)

Myers, Walter Dean. *145th Street Short Stories.* Delacorte Press, 2000. ISBN 0-385-32137-6

Life on 145th Street in Harlem is hard, and you have to take it seriously. These ten stories all took place on 145th Street. They include Big Joe's funeral, a Christmas story, monkeyman, and block party—145th Street style. (7–12)

Nonfiction

Bang, Molly. *Common Ground: The Water, Earth, and Air We Share.* Blue Sky Press, 1997. ISBN 0-590-10056-4

If mankind continues to use as much of our natural resources as they want, man may end up destroying the whole world. Therefore, we have a responsibility to conserve our resources because if we destroy the earth, there is no other place to go. (3–7)

Blue, Rose, and Corinne J. Naden. *Colin Powell.* Millbrook Press, 1997. ISBN 0-7613-0242-5

Colin Powell found "a home in the army." Early on he is recognized as a leader and eventually becomes a four star general. He is named chairman of the Joint Chiefs of Staff and oversees Operation Desert Storm in 1990–1991. (2–4)

_____. *People of Peace.* Millbrook Press, 1994. ISBN 1-56294-409-6

This is the inspirational story of eleven people who work for peace in the world. They include Andrew Carnegie, Jane Addams, Woodrow Wilson, Mohandas [sic] Gandhi, Ralph Bunche, Dag Hammarskjold, Jimmy Carter, Desmond Tutu, Oscar Arias Sanchez, Betty Williams, and Mairead Corrigan Maguire. (4–6)

 The more cooperative the group, the greater is the fitness for survival which extends to all of its members.
—Ashley Montague

Connolly, Sean. *Neil Armstrong.* Heinemann Library, 1998. ISBN 1-5757-2692-0

On July 20, 1969, Neil Armstrong walks on the moon, the result of a team effort. "That's one small step for man, one giant leap for mankind." (4–6)

Guiberson, Brenda Z. *The Emperor Lays an Egg.* Henry Holt, 2001. ISBN 0-8050-6204-1

One year in the life of an emperor penguin, from laying the egg by the female, taking care of the egg by the male, feeding the chick by both, and then mating to start the whole process all over again. (00–3)

Hoose, Phillip. *It's Our World, Too!* Little, Brown and Company, 1993. ISBN 0-316-37241-2

This book begins with a brief history of young activists who make a difference. Next the stories of fourteen children and teens with concerns, energy, and commitment are profiled. The last part of this book is a handbook for young people who want to plan for and initiate a change. (5–10)

Robinson, Sharon. *Jackie's Nine: Jackie Robinson's Values to Live By*. Scholastic, 2001. ISBN 0-439-23764-5

> The author, the daughter of Jackie Robinson, picks nine values that celebrate his life. Each chapter is devoted to one of these values and depicts a scene from both lives to illustrate the principle along with the life of one of her heroes. In her chapter on teamwork, Sharon demonstrates how her educational program, Breaking Barriers, based on the nine values, brings hope and change in one little boy's life. (6–8)

Slavin, Ed. *Jimmy Carter*. Chelsea House, 1988. ISBN 0-791-00560-7

> The thirty-ninth president of the United States was Jimmy Carter, who was born in the small town of Plains, Georgia. He attended the U.S. Naval Academy and married Rosalynn Smith when he graduated. As president, Carter negotiated a peace treaty between Israel and Egypt. Jimmy Carter's administration saw many highs and lows, but he is known for his peace effort. (7–12)

Chapter *10*

Tolerance

Related Virtues

Acceptance, patience, equality, justice, moderation, mercy, and temperance

Definition

The capacity for or the practice of recognizing and respecting the beliefs or practices of others

Tolerance in Action

    ♦ Be accepting of others who are not like you.

    ♦ Be understanding of those with different beliefs or who are from different cultures.

    ♦ Be patient with classmates who are not as capable as you are.

    ♦ Treat others fairly.

    ♦ Help to make sure that justice prevails.

    ♦ Play computer games in moderation.

    ♦ Show mercy in dealing with your classmates.

    ♦ Have patience with younger siblings.

People Who Have Demonstrated This Virtue

    ♦ Coretta Scott King

    ♦ Susan B. Anthony

    ♦ Marie Curie

    ♦ Babe Didrikson Zaharias

    ♦ Amelia Earhart

⟡ Ben Franklin

⟡ Ruby Bridges

Discussion Questions

⟡ Does your concept of fairness change?

⟡ Would getting to know a person better help you to be more tolerant?

⟡ Will there be a time when everything is fair?

⟡ Is being different a bad thing?

⟡ Why is it important to be tolerant of others?

⟡ Are all laws fair to all people?

⟡ How do you feel when you are being treated unfairly? What can you do?

Related Topics to Explore

⟡ Ethnicity

⟡ Multiculturalism

⟡ Japanese internment

⟡ Holocaust

⟡ Prejudice

⟡ Ku Klux Klan

⟡ Equal Rights Amendment

⟡ Title IX Funding for women's sports in higher education

⟡ The U.S. court system

Annotated Titles

Picture Books

Bunting, Eve. *The Days of Summer.* Harcourt, 2001. ISBN 0-15-201840-9

    Nora and Jo-Jo's grandparents are getting a divorce. The sisters find this very distressing and try to get their grandparents to stay together. In the end, they find that they can cope with this new and upsetting situation because each grandparent makes special efforts to spend time with them. (K–4)

Falconer, Ian. *Olivia.* Atheneum Children's Books, 2000. ISBN 0-689-82953-1

    Olivia is a pig with endless energy. She loves the color red, and when she tries to decide what to wear, she tries on every single outfit in her closet. She admires paintings at the Metropolitan Museum of Art and comes home to create her own work of art on the wall. When she goes to the beach, she builds a sandcastle that resembles a New York City skyscraper. She always totally exhausts her mother. (ps–3)

Fox, Mem. *Harriet, You'll Drive Me Wild.* Harcourt Children's Books, 2003. ISBN 0-15-204598-8
     Preschooler Harriet Harris is always making a mess—spilling and dripping everything. Her mother's blood pressure rises, and she yells a lot. Harriet says she sorry after these things happen. Harriet and her mother can get upset, but they know they will always love each other. (ps–2)

McKissack, Patricia C. *Goin' Someplace Special.* Atheneum Children's Books, 2001. ISBN 0-689-81885-8
     In segregated Nashville, in the early 1950s, 'Tricia Ann asks her grandmother if she can go someplace special. Her grandmother is not sure that she wants 'Tricia Ann to go off by herself but finally lets her go. On her walk through town, she is chased from a hotel lobby, then she is reminded that she cannot enter the movie theater through the front door and that she must sit way up in the balcony. But she eventually gets to the place where she is welcome—that special someplace is the public library. (ps–3)

McPhail, David. *Mole Music.* Henry Holt, 2001. ISBN 0-8050-6766-3
     Mole spends his time digging underground all by himself. One night while watching television, he hears a musician playing the violin and wishes he could make those sweet sounds, too. He begins with the usual squealing and squeaking, but eventually his efforts become melodic. The illustrations show how Mole's years of practice and resulting sweet music have affected the animals and humans around him. (00–5)

Rylant, Cynthia. *Little Whistle.* Harcourt Children's Books, 2003. ISBN 0-15-204762-X
     Little Whistle is a guinea pig who lives in a toy store. Every evening when Toytown closes, Little Whistle wakes up, puts on his blue pea coat, and plays with his friends, the toys. (ps–2)

Primary (grades 1–3)

Nolen, Jerdine. *Raising Dragons.* Harcourt Brace, 1998. ISBN 0-15-201288-5
     A little girl goes for a walk with her father, and they find a big egg in Miller's cave. She is told to stay away, but she just has to check on that egg everyday until finally a tiny dragon pokes its head out. She names him Hank, feeds him, and reads to him at night. The dragon turns out to be an asset to the farm. Soon Hank draws a lot of attention and crowds of people. The little girl directs Hank to an island in the middle of the ocean where there are dragons everywhere. When it is time for the little girl to board her plane alone, Hank loads her up with dragon eggs, because she knows so much about raising dragons. (ps–3)

 Anger and intolerance are the twin enemies of correct understanding.
     —Mahatma Gandhi

Park, Barbara. *Junie B. First Grader: Toothless Wonder.* Random House, 2003. ISBN 0-375-80295-9
     Junie is the first one in the first grade to have a wiggly front tooth. She is very concerned about her appearance when the tooth finally comes out. And she is worried about the Tooth Fairy. Who is this lady? What does she do with all the teeth she takes from little kids? (1–4)

Uhlberg, Myron. *Dad, Jackie, and Me.* Peachtree, 2005. ISBN 1-56145-329-3
     A young boy and his father, who is deaf, follow the career of Jackie Robinson. His father, who has suffered prejudice, learns as much as he can about Jackie. He even tries to play catch but is unable to catch a ball. That changes during the last Dodgers game. Jackie catches the last out of the game and tosses the ball into the stands. That's when dad reaches up and catches the ball bare-handed, a first. (2–5)

Woodson, Jacqueline. *The Other Side.* G. P. Putnam's Sons, 2001. ISBN 0-399-23116-1

> Two girls, one white and one black, are separated by a fence, and each keeps to her side. One day, Clover approaches the fence and meets Annie. They spend the summer getting to know each other while sitting on the fence. (00–up)

Intermediate (grades 3–5)

Avi. *Ereth's Birthday.* HarperCollins, 2001. ISBN 0-380-80490-5

> Ereth is a porcupine who lives in Dimwood Forest and is convinced that his friends have forgotten his birthday. So he goes off in search of salt, his favorite treat. Instead, he finds a mother fox dying in a hunter's trap. She begs him to look after her three kits, and he agrees. He soon realizes that looking after three growing fox kits is no easy task. (3–7)

Blume, Judy. *Double Fudge.* Penguin, 2003. ISBN 0-14-250111-5

> Peter Hatcher is now entering the seventh grade, and five-year-old Fudge is currently obsessed with money—he has even created his own Fudge Bucks. The family takes a trip to Washington, D.C., to visit the Bureau of Printing and Engraving, and they meet Mr. Hatcher's long lost cousin, Howie and his family. They come to Manhattan to visit the Hatchers and they stay with them in their crowded apartment. Cousin Howie's children, twin girls named Flora and Fauna and four-year-old Farley, become a great source of embarrassment for Peter. (3–5)

Brown, Jackie. *Little Cricket.* Hyperion, 2004. ISBN 0-7868-1852-2

> The North Vietnamese soldiers drive twelve-year-old Kia Vang out of her small village and they flee to Thailand. Because of a mix-up, Kia's mother and grandmother are left behind when her brother, grandfather, and Kia emigrate to St. Paul, Minnesota. Kia's brother Xigi loses the Laotian ways, spends little time in the apartment, and is unwilling to help Kia and her grandfather. Kia makes friends with Hank and her son, Sam, who are very kind to her. Grandfather reminds Kia that people "must learn to trust each other to make our lives good." (4–7)

Bruchac, Joseph. *The Arrow over the Door.* Dial Books for Young Readers, 1998. ISBN 0-8037-2078-5

> This story is told through two differing viewpoints in alternating chapters. Samuel is fourteen years old and a Quaker; he is having mixed feelings about his society's stance on nonviolence. Stands Straight is a Abenaki Indian whose mother and brother are killed by a group of drunken white people. The English ask the Abenaki to attack the Americans. The Abenaki come upon the Quakers when they are together at a meeting. Stands Straight notices that the people are unarmed and that they leave the door partially open to show that all are welcome. The Indians bravely enter the cabin and feel welcome. Both Samuel and Stands Straight have a change of heart as they exchange friendship. (4–6)

Curtis, Christopher Paul. *The Watsons Go to Birmingham—1963: A Novel.* Delacorte Press, 1995. ISBN 0-385-32175-9

> This story is narrated by Kenny, nine years old, about his middle-class black family, the weird Watsons of Flint, Michigan. Kenny's thirteen-year-old brother, Byron, keeps getting into more and more trouble. The family decides to visit grandma in Birmingham because she is the only one who can make an impression on Byron. They happen to be in Birmingham when Grandma's church is blown up. (4–7)

Gantos, Jack. *Joey Pigza Swallowed the Key.* HarperCollins, 2000. ISBN 0-06-449267-2

> "Joey Pigza is wired. Really wired." Joey's actions are unpredictable and spontaneous. When he is on medication, Joey is focused, but when it is no longer effective he may swallow his household key or walk on the highest beam in a barn on a school field trip. Because Joey is endangering himself and others, he is sent to the Lancaster County Special Education Center for

further evaluation. Will Joey get the help he needs for his physical and mental well-being? Will he ever return to regular school? (4–6)

Park, Linda Sue. *The Kite Fighters*. Clarion Books, 2000. ISBN 0-395-94041-9
In the year 1473 in Korea, there live two brothers, Young-sup and Kee-sup. The brothers are very good at making and flying kites. The young king of Korea comes to them for help with making and flying a kite. He then wants them to fly a kite for him in the New Years Kite Fighters contest. (4–7)

Polacco, Patricia. *The Butterfly*. Philomel, 2000. ISBN 0-399-23170-6
The Nazis march into a small French village and terrorize all inhabitants including little Monique. Monique dreams of a little ghost child sitting on her bed and wakes to discover the little girl is real. She is Sevrine, a Jewish girl, who is hiding with her family in the basement. Monique and Sevrine become good friends until the Nazis discover them, and both families have to run for their lives. This book is based on a true story. (1–5, for older readers)

 Nothing dies so hard, or rallies so often as intolerance.
—Henry Ward Beecher

Pryor, Bonnie. *Joseph 1861—A Rumble of War*. HarperCollins, 2000. ISBN 0-380-73103-7
Joseph is from a small town in Kentucky and the story takes place just before the Civil War. Joseph's stepfather is an abolitionist yet Joseph grows up with slaves in his household. He is faced with a dilemma when he discovers two runaway slaves in his barn. (3–6)

Seidler, Tor. *Mean Margaret*. HarperCollins, 2001. ISBN 0-06-441039-0
Fred and Phoebe are a recently married woodchuck couple. Fred is expecting to continue his orderly life. But Phoebe finds a deserted child, adopts her, and calls her Margaret, after her mother. Life is not the same with Margaret around because she wrecks their home, eats all their food, and grows and grows. In the end, Margaret finds her family, and Phoebe and Fred get to settle down with their new woodchuck baby, Patience. (2–4)

Middle School (grades 5–8)

Bunting, Eve. *Spying on Miss Muller*. Ballantine Books, 1996. ISBN 0-449-70455-6
During World War II, Miss Muller is thankful for her teaching job at an English boarding school. Her father was a Nazi officer, now deceased, and her mother is English. Miss Muller is the girl's favorite teacher. Then the English go to war with Germany and the girls become suspicious of her when they discover her leaving her room at night. Jessie follows Miss Muller and searches her room for evidence about her father. The girls continue to follow Miss Muller, with surprising results. From Miss Mueller Jessie learns that when you love someone, you do not have to agree with all that they do, and it is wrong to feel ashamed of them. (5–7)

Lester, Julius. *Day of Tears: A Novel in Dialogue*. Hyperion, 2005. ISBN 0-7868-0490-0
This story is told completely in dialogue by three of the people involved in the largest slave auction in America. The three characters are a slave, a master, and a slave seller. The story revolves around twelve-year-old Emma, a slave who works for the master in his house and takes care of his two children. The slave seller is sure that Emma will bring a good price. (5–8)

Lynch, Chris. *Gold Dust*. HarperCollins, 2000. ISBN 0-06-028174-X
The story takes place in 1975 in Boston, when the Gold Dust Twins, Jim Rice and Fred Lynn, play for the Red Sox. Seventh-grader Richard Moncreif thinks only of baseball until a new student from the Dominican Republic enrolls at his parochial school. Napoleon Ellis is black, upper

middle class, well-spoken, and plays cricket; the two boys become friends. Richard has a dream that they will become the next Gold Dust Twins for the Red Sox. However, Napoleon does not share that dream, and the racial tensions caused by the 1975 Boston busing controversy eventually destroy their friendship. (5–8)

 The greatest problem in the world today is intolerance. Everyone is so intolerant of each other.
—Princess of Wales Diana

Park, Linda Sue. *Project Mulberry.* Houghton Mifflin, 2005. ISBN 0-618-47786-1
   Julia Song, a seventh grader and the only Korean at her school, and her friend Patrick decide to raise silkworms for their science project. They hope to win a blue ribbon in the state fair. Julia, however, is concerned about the way the project might be accepted at the fair—she wants an American project, but this is a Korean project. The author alternates a chapter of story with a chapter of conversation between Julia and the author talking about writing the story and developing the characters. (5–9)

Salisbury, Graham. *Under the Blood Red Sun.* Bantam Doubleday Dell, 1995. ISBN 0-440-41139-4
   The setting is Hawaii and the story tells of Tomi and his Japanese American family just before the bombing of Pearl Harbor in 1941. The family suffers racism, hostility, and adversity. Scott O'Dell Award winner for historical fiction. (5–8)

Wisler, G. Clifton. *Caleb's Choice.* Dutton Children's Books, 1996. ISBN 0-525-67526-4
   Caleb's dad is having major money problems, so Caleb leaves his private school and travels alone across Texas to live with his grandmother. In the 1850s in Texas, a law makes it a crime for anyone to help a runaway slave. So when an escaped slave saves Caleb's life, he has to make up his mind as to whether he will join his cousin and grandmother who are secretly aiding runaway slaves. (4–7)

YA (grades 8–12)

Chotjewitz, David. *Daniel Half Human and the Good Nazi.* Atheneum Children's Books, 2004. ISBN 0-689-85747-0
   This is a flashback from the point of view of Daniel, the main character. As an adult, he goes back to Hamburg as an American interpreter, and he remembers 1933, the year he lived in Hamburg and attended a German school. Gradually the situation in the country deteriorated, and Daniel was told he was half Jewish. He maintained his relationship with his German friend, Armin, who warned him of the upcoming Kristallnacht. Daniel was one of the last people to leave Germany for the United States, leaving behind his cousin and uncle. Armin protected himself by acting inhumanely to the Jewish people. He became a member of the Hitler Youth and the Nazi Party. Back in the present, Daniel holds Armin's life in his hands the same way Armin held his family's lives in his hands in 1933. (7–up)

Cormier, Robert. *The Rag and Bone Shop.* Delacorte Press, 2001. ISBN 0-385-72962-6
   Twelve-year-old Jason is the last to see his seven-year-old neighbor alive. She is brutally murdered, her body found covered with leaves in the woods. It is a high-profile case with no evidence, but the police call in a well-know interrogator named Trent, who always gets a confession. When Jason meets Trent, he thinks he is helping. His father is away on a business trip, and his mother lets him go off with the police assuring him that he has a duty to assist. The end results are devastating for both Trent and Jason. (7–up)

Crowe, Chris. *Mississippi Trial, 1955*. Dial Books for Young Readers, 2002. ISBN 0-14-250192-1

This is a fictional account of the murder of Emmett Till, a black teenager from Chicago. The story is told through the eyes of Hiram who can't understand why his own father does not want to visit his family and hometown of Greenwood, Mississippi. At first Hiram is excited about visiting his grandfather, but after participating in a racial confrontation, he begins to understand his father's thinking. When Hiram attempts to share his leftover lunch with Emmett, R. C. a local bully, forces Emmett to the ground. R. C. humiliates him by cutting open a fish and stuffing the innards into Emmett's mouth. Hiram is ashamed of himself because he stands by and lets it happen, while Emmett thinks Hiram is a friend despite the difference in color. Emmett is tortured and murdered for whistling at a white woman, but the thinking at the time among whites in Mississippi is that he brought it on himself. (6–8)

Freymann-Weyr, Garret. *My Heartbeat*. Houghton Mifflin, 2002. ISBN 0-618-14181-4

The triangle of James, Link, and Ellen changes when Ellen attempts to really get to know her brother. She asks Link if he and James are a couple. This sets off a chain reaction. Link starts dating Polly, which pleases his father so much that he gives Link an extra allowance. Ellen has always been attracted to James, and they become a couple. Ellen knows that James has had relations with other men and that he probably will have both men and women in his future. Ellen realizes that one can only know another person—for example, Link or James—just so much; there are some things one can never know. (7–12, for mature readers)

Jordan, Sherryl. *The Raging Quiet*. Simon & Schuster, 1999. ISBN 0-8050-5599-1

Marne is unafraid of work and attracts the attention of the lord's middle son. When her father suffers a stroke and is unable to work, Marne agrees to marry Isake so that her family can remain in the overseer's house. Isake and Marne relocate to the fishing hamlet of Torcurra. Isake falls to his death from the roof of their little cottage. Marne befriends a youth that everyone, except the kindly priest, thinks is a madman. Marne learns that he is not mad but deaf. She develops a sign language so that they are able to communicate. The local townspeople are suspicious of anyone who is different. They believe that Marne is a witch who put a curse on her late husband and converses with Raven, the madman. They put her on trial as a witch. How will she be able to survive the trial ahead? This tale belongs to any time, even our own; it is about prejudice and ignorance and a young woman wrongly accused; Marne is guilty of only one thing—the unforgivable crime of being different. (7–up)

Krisher, Trudy. *Spite Fences*. Delacorte Press, 1994. ISBN 0-385-32088-4

Maggie Pugh lives in Kinship, Georgia. She receives her first camera from Zeke who buys and sells his wares on the main street. The camera allows Maggie to see beyond the lens into the thoughts and hearts of her family and people she grew up with, both black and white. Zeke also is instrumental in getting Maggie a job cleaning house for George Hardy, a black civil rights lawyer who lives outside of town. During the summer of 1960, Maggie witnesses an inhumane act inflicted on Zeke, initiated by Vigil Boggs, her neighbor. It is a summer of civil rights and resistance and Maggie is the key to the changes ahead. (7–12)

Myers, Walter Dean. *Monster*. HarperCollins, 1999. ISBN 0-06-028077-8

Sixteen-year-old Steve Harmon is on trial for felony murder. The prosecutor calls him a monster because of his role in the murder of a convenience store owner. But was Steve really the lookout for those involved in a robbery? Steve wants to write screenplays for films, so he records his impressions of the trial, the crime scene, and his jail time in movie-script layout alternating with journal entries, presented in a typeface resembling handwriting in the book. (7–up)

Nixon, Joan Lowery. *Nobody's There*. Bantam Doubleday Dell, 2000. ISBN 0-385-32567-3

Abbie Thompson is very angry at her father. He has left the family for a younger woman, and now her mother is depressed and her younger brother is angry. Abbie is arrested after throwing rocks through the girlfriend's window. As her punishment, she is assigned to look after a bad-tempered old woman, Mrs. Merkel, who is part of a group trying to put an end to scams on senior citizens. When Mrs. Merkel is attacked and hospitalized, it is up to Abbie to try to find out who did it based on illegible scribbling that Mrs. Merkel left in an old notebook. (6–9)

Shusterman, Neal. *The Dark Side of Nowhere: A Novel.* Little, Brown and Company, 1997. ISBN 0-316-78907-0
  Fourteen-year-old Jason Miller describes his town and life as incredibly dull. But when his best friend dies of apparent appendicitis, things start to change dramatically. Jason learns that his best friend didn't really die but has been transformed into an alien. His parents are aliens, and his friends are training for an alien invasion, which will be the second attempt, the first one having failed, leaving them alone on Earth. (7–12)

Wilson, Diane Lee. *I Rode a Horse of Milk White Jade.* Orchard, 1998. ISBN 0-531-30024-2
  Oyuna was born on the Mongolian steppes during the reign of Kublai Khan. As an infant, Oyuna's foot is crushed by a horse, and her family believes she is cursed. When she is thirteen years old, she sets off on a journey disguised as a boy with her white mare and her cat. Oyuna has a special gift with horses; she can hear them speak. She goes in search of the perfect white horse belonging to Kublai Khan so that she can win a race. The story is told by an elderly Oyuna to her granddaughter as they await the birth of a foal that is the direct descendent of Oyuna's beloved mare in the story. (6–10)

The highest result of education is tolerance.
—Helen Keller

Nonfiction

Coles, Robert. *The Story of Ruby Bridges.* Scholastic, 1995. ISBN 0-590-43967-7
  In 1960, Ruby Bridges was one of four black girls sent to two all-white New Orleans schools by court order. Ruby attended the first grade at Frantz Elementary School. Federal marshals were sent to accompany Ruby and protect her from people who did not want the schools integrated. Ruby was the only child in the school; the white parents would not send their children to school. Ruby was brave, facing the angry mobs day after day. Every day Ruby prayed for the people who were so angry, and later in the year children gradually came back to school. (1–4)

Cox, Clinton. *Come All You Brave Soldiers: Blacks in the Revolutionary War.* Scholastic, 1999. ISBN 0-590-47576-2
  More than five thousand blacks joined the Continental Army during the Revolutionary War. The author retells the history of the war including details about the blacks who joined the army freely and those who were forced. (5–9)

Freedman, Russell. *The Voice That Challenged a Nation: Marian Anderson and the Struggle for Equal Rights.* Clarion Books, 2004. ISBN 0-618-15976-5
  Marian Anderson did not set out to be a symbol of civil rights. She was born in 1897 in South Philadelphia. Her father died when she was quite young, forcing her mother, Marian, and her two sisters to move in with the girls' grandparents. When she finished grade school, there was no money for high school or music lessons, so her first voice teacher was a well-known local black soprano who refused payment. Later, when Marian traveled as a professional singer in the segregated South, she was not allowed to stay in some hotels, and the audiences were segregated. As her audiences grew larger, her sponsors asked that she sing at the Daughters of the American Revolution (DAR) Auditorium in Washington, D.C. But it was against the organization's policy to allow a black to perform at the auditorium. The first lady, Eleanor Roosevelt, resigned from

the DAR when Marian was not allowed to sing there. Her supporters were not discouraged; instead, they made arrangements for her to sing standing on the steps of the Lincoln Memorial to a crowd of seventy-five thousand people. (5–9)

Hansen, Joyce. *Women of Hope: African Americans Who Made a Difference.* Scholastic, 1998. ISBN 0-590-93973-4

Full-page posters and accompanying one-page text describe thirteen "women of color whose persistence and vision gave society hopefulness and inspiration—an inspiration we still see today." The women featured include Ida B. Wells-Barnett, the Delany sisters, Septima Poinsette Clark, Ella Josephine Baker, Fannie Lou Hamer, Ruby Dee, Maya Angelou, Toni Morrison, Marian Wright Edelman, Alice Walker, Alexa Canady, and Mae C. Jeminson. Additional women of hope are divided by professions and included for further study at the end of the book. (3–7)

Linder, Greg. *Marie Curie.* Bridgestone Books, 1999. ISBN 0-7368-0206-1

World famous physicist Madame Curie discovered radium and radiation. With her husband, Pierre, they won the Nobel Prize in physics. Eight years later, Marie won the Nobel Prize in chemistry. Their discoveries have saved many lives. (1–5)

Moss, Marissa. *Mighty Jackie: The Strike-Out Queen.* Simon & Schuster, 2004. ISBN 0-689-86329-2

This is the true story of Jackie Mitchell, a seventeen-year-old girl, who pitched for the Chattanooga Lookouts. In 1931, they played the New York Yankees. Jackie's hard work over the years came into play when she struck out the mighty Babe Ruth and Lou Gehrig. (K–3)

The test of courage comes when we are in the minority; the test of tolerance comes when we are in the majority.
—Ralph W. Sockman

Nieuwsma, Milton J. *Kinderlager: An Oral History of Young Holocaust Survivors.* Holiday House, 1998. ISBN 0-8234-1358-6

Kinderlager was a special section of the Auschwitz-Birkenau concentration camp that houses children. This book documents the lives of three of these children at various times—before the war, in the concentration camp, during liberation by the Soviets, and after the war. At the time of the Soviet liberation, the world did not take much notice of the children who been held in the camps. This is the true story of three of the youngest survivors of Kinderlager. (6–up)

Pinkney, Andrea Davis. *Let It Shine: Stories of Black Women Freedom Fighters.* Gulliver Books, 2000. ISBN 0-15-201005-X

These are the stories of ten female black freedom fighters from the eighteenth century to the present day. The women all have something in common: they speak out for what they believe in an unequal world. Including in the volume are Sojourner Truth, Biddy Mason, Harriet Tubman, Ida B. Wells-Barnett, Mary McLeod Bethune, Ella Josephine Baker, Dorothy Irene Height, Rosa Parks, Fannie Lou Hamer, and Shirley Chisholm. (4–7)

Press, Petra. *Coretta Scott King.* Heinemann Library, 2000. ISBN 1-575-72496-0

Coretta Scott King continued to fight for civil rights of poor people and minorities long after her husband, Martin Luther King, Jr., was shot and killed. She continued to fight for peace and human rights through nonviolent protest and the highest principles of law and order. (4–7)

Roop, Peter, and Connie Roop. *Benjamin Franklin.* Scholastic Reference, 2000. ISBN 0-439-15806-0
   The primary sources of Ben Franklin's autobiography, letters, and writings were used for this biography. Ben Franklin, writer, printer, inventor, scientist, and diplomat, was one of the most important men of the American Revolution. (3–6)

Ryan, Pam Muñoz. *When Marian Sang.* Scholastic Press, 2002. ISBN 0-439-26967-9
   Marian Anderson grew up in south Philadelphia. As her reputation as a singer grew, members of her church promised to pay her tuition if she was accepted to a music school. When she went to the school to ask about admission, she was first ignored and then told that colored were not accepted. This shocked Marian; she had thought that music transcended prejudice. Marian continued to sing at churches and was invited to sing to separate audiences, one black and one white. When she went to audition with the famous Giuseppe Boghetti, a master singing coach, Marian was told that he did not have room for any new students. But then Marian simply began to sing, and at the sound of her voice, she was accepted immediately. She traveled to Europe and performed in many concert halls; there she faced much less discrimination. When she returned to the United States in 1939, however, she was again faced with prejudice. Many halls were closed to her because of policies that allowed only white performers. When she was barred from performing at one venue in Washington, D.C., it was decided that the only place large enough to hold her audience would be the steps of the Lincoln Memorial. It was Easter Morning. Marian was afraid that no one would come. Instead, she sang before an audience of seventy-five thousand people. She closed the program with a spiritual: "Oh, nobody knows the trouble I see, Nobody knows my sorrow...." (1–5)

 Tolerance it a tremendous virtue, but the immediate neighbors of tolerance are apathy and weakness.
   —James Goldsmith

Tillage, Leon Walter. *Leon's Story.* Farrar, Straus & Giroux, 1997. ISBN 0-374-44330-0
   This is the story of Leon Walter Tillage as spoken on tape to Susan L. Roth. Leon currently works as a custodian at the Park School in Baltimore, Maryland, where he gives a speech about his life as a part of the curriculum. Leon was the son of a sharecropper and grew up in North Carolina in the 1940s. His young life was about hard work and getting an education in an inferior school. It was about walking home from school and being passed by the white kids in the bus who hollered and called him names. When this happened, the black children ran and tried to hide, but sometimes the bus stopped, and the white kids would get off and throw stones at whomever they could. Leon witnesses his father being intentionally run over and killed by drunken white teenagers, who were never punished for their actions. "In those days, blacks didn't have any voice at all, and there was no such thing as taking the white man to court. You couldn't vote; you weren't even considered a citizen." (4–up)

Yoo, Paula. *Sixteen Years in Sixteen Seconds: The Sammy Lee Story.* Lee and Low Books, 2005. ISBN 1-58430-247-X
   Sammy lived up to his father's words: "In America, you can achieve anything if you set your heart to it." He became a champion diver despite the fact he was of Asian descent and therefore discriminated against. For example, he was allowed to swim only on those days when people of color were permitted at the pool. In 1948, Sammy won bronze and gold medals for diving. (K–3)

Chapter *11*

Citizenship

Related Virtues

Activism, participation, community service, love of freedom, patriotism, leadership

Definition

The status of a citizen with its attendant duties, rights, and privileges, the quality of an individual's behavior as a citizen

Citizenship in Action

⬦ Be proud of your heritage.

⬦ Be proud of your country.

⬦ Be aware of your rights and the rights of others.

⬦ Participate in community service.

⬦ Be a leader at school.

⬦ Write a letter to your senator or representative.

⬦ Encourage adults you know to vote.

⬦ Be politically active.

⬦ Display the flag properly.

People Who Have Demonstrated This Virtue

⬦ Jacques Cousteau

⬦ Mary McLeod Bethune

⬦ Solon

✧ Hammurabi

✧ Barbara Jordan

✧ Ralph Nadar

✧ Julia Butterfly Hill

✧ Nelson Mandela

✧ Sun Yat-Sen

✧ Martin Luther King, Jr.

Discussion Questions

✧ How can you get involved in your community?

✧ Why is it important to be a good citizen?

✧ What do all communities have in common?

✧ Why is it necessary to have laws?

✧ How are laws created?

✧ Why is freedom important?

✧ How can you exercise your freedom?

✧ Should people have the freedom to do whatever they want?

Related Topics to Explore

✧ Service projects

✧ Law making process

✧ Right to vote

✧ Writing letters to the editor

✧ Patriotic symbols

✧ Amnesty International

✧ United States Humane Society

✧ Flag display

Annotated Titles

Picture Books

Borden, Louise. *The Little Ships: The Heroic Rescue at Dunkirk in World War II.* Margaret K. McElderry Books, 1997. ISBN 0-689-80827-5

A little girl and her dad cross the English Channel to help to rescue Allied troops from the Nazis at Dunkirk. They are in their fishing boat, and they connect with other regular citizens in their small boats in this heroic effort. (4–up)

Bunting, Eve. *A Picnic in October.* Harcourt Brace, 1999. ISBN 0-15-201656-2

Every year Tony and his family meet his grandparents, cousins, and extended family, and they take the ferry to the Statue of Liberty. They spread a blanket on the grass and have a picnic under the watchful eyes of Lady Liberty. Tony at first is embarrassed when they light the birthday candles and grandma blows them out. Especially when they all blow kisses to Lady Liberty as grandma gives thanks for taking her in. But then when Tony sees some new Americans standing in solemn reverence, he gets a sense of his grandmother's feelings. (K–3)

Grodin, Elissa. *D Is for Democracy: A Citizen's Alphabet.* Sleeping Bear Press, 2004. ISBN 1-58536-284-4

This ABC book includes the major symbols of democracy along with a further description in a sidebar. For example, B is for Bill of Rights and J is for Judicial Branch, with extensive discussion. (1–3)

Levitin, Sonia. *Nine for California.* Orchard, 1996. ISBN 0-531-09527-4

This story provides information about the stagecoaches of the 1800s. A little girl and her siblings and mother take the long stagecoach ride from Missouri to California, where the father and husband is waiting for them to start a new life. (ps–3)

Scillian, Devin. *One Nation: America by the Numbers.* Sleeping Bear Press, 2002. ISBN 1-58536-249-2

Each number 1–15, 20, 50, and 100 represent a symbol of America. For example, the number 20 is a score, and the Gettysburg Address begins with "Four score and seven years ago…." (1–3)

Van Leeuwen, Jean. *Across the Wide Dark Sea: The Mayflower Journey.* Dial Books for Young Readers, 1996. ISBN 0-8037-1166-2

A boy and his father travel on the Mayflower to the new land. The trip is very, very difficult, and it takes nine weeks. When they arrive, it is cold and snowflakes are falling. They find a place to build a cabin and make friends with the Indians who assist them with the planting of the corn. (K–3)

Primary (grades 1–3)

Cohen, Barbara. *Molly's Pilgrim.* HarperCollins, 1998. ISBN 0-688-16279-7

Molly does not like her new school because the girls make fun of her language and her Jewish heritage. Molly has immigrated to the United States from Russia. In November, her class studies Thanksgiving, and everyone is asked to bring in a pilgrim doll. Molly's mother makes a doll that looks just like Molly when she first came to the United States. The children make fun of her doll, so the teacher intervenes and explains that her doll is a modern pilgrim. (1–4)

Hoff, Syd. *The Horse in Harry's Room.* HarperTrophy, 2000. ISBN 0-06-444073-7

Harry has a horse in his room that only he can see. His parents take him to see real horses that run free, and then Harry wonders whether his horse should be free, too. (0–3)

Lee, Milly. *Nim and the War Effort.* Farrar, Straus & Giroux, 1997. ISBN 0-374-35523-1

Nim collects newspapers to take to school for the paper drive. Nim is in luck and finds a whole room full of newspapers. How will she get them to school before the contest ends? She finds a way, but her actions disgrace her Chinese family. (2–4)

Le Guin, Ursula K. *Jane on Her Own.* Orchard, 1999. ISBN 0-531-30133-8

Jane is a cat with wings who leaves home to see the world. She is taken in by a man who treats her royally but traps her inside while he makes money exploiting her amazing wings on television. Jane escapes and makes it back home to stay with her mother and the wonderful lady they live with who understands her need for a home and a little freedom. (1–4)

Miller, Sara Swan. *Three Stories You Can Read to Your Dog.* Houghton Mifflin, 1995. ISBN 0-395-69938-X

> Each story is addressed to a dog. One is about a burglar, one about bones, and the last is about running free. (K–3)

Ransom, Candice F. *Rescue on the Outer Banks.* Carolrhoda Books, 2002. ISBN 0-87614-460-1

> The Pea Island Life-Saving station was manned by an African American crew on the Outer Banks of North Carolina. This fictional story is based on the account of the Pea Island crew rescue of the *E. S. Newman* passengers and crew in 1896. (1–3)

Sachar, Louis. *Class President.* Random House, 1999. ISBN 0-679-88999-X

> Marvin's school is wearing clothes with holes in them on "hole day" when the president of the United States, along with reporters, makes a surprise visit. The president asks questions of the class and makes statements about being a citizen. (1–4)

 Citizenship consists in the service of the country.
—Jawaharlal Nehru

Intermediate (grades 3–5)

Bennett, William J. *The Children's Book of America.* Simon & Schuster Trade, 1998. ISBN 0-684-84930-5

> This book embodies the spirit of America in the selected stories, legends, songs, and poems. Share these experiences, ideals, and aspirations with children so that they understand the principles and character we revere as a nation. (4–7)

Brill, Marlene Targ. *Diary of a Drummer Boy.* Millbrook Press, 1998. ISBN 0-7613-0118-6

> This is the fictional diary of Orion Howe who becomes a drummer along with his brother, Lyston, in the Civil War when they are not even thirteen years old. Because of his bravery at Vicksburg, Orion receives the Congressional Medal of Honor. (2–5)

Hermes, Patricia. *Our Strange New Land.* Scholastic, 2000. ISBN 0-439-11208-7

> Nine boats leave Plymouth and only four arrive in Jamestown, Virginia, after surviving a hurricane at sea. Elizabeth writes in her diary about meeting Captain John Smith, Pocahontas, and Indians, and about the hard work, illness, and sorrow. (3–5)

Turner, Ann. *Drummer Boy: Marching to the Civil War.* HarperCollins, 1998. ISBN 0-06-027696-7

> A young boy is influenced by Abraham Lincoln; he decides to lie about his age and join the Union in the Civil War. He becomes a drummer boy to help put spirit into the soldiers. The individual battles begin to run together, and he sees "things no boy should ever see." (2–4)

Middle School (grades 5–8)

Elliott, L. M. *Under a War-Torn Sky.* Hyperion, 2001. ISBN 0-786-80755-5

> American Henry Forester, a Royal Air Force pilot during World War II, is shot down on a bombing mission. He has many adventures as he makes his way back through Nazi-occupied Europe and meets members of the French resistance. (7–9)

Fogelin, Adrian. *Crossing Jordan.* Peachtree, 2000. ISBN 1-56145-215-7

> When Jemmie, an African American, moves next door to Cass, the two become friends in spite of their family's racist objections. The situation improves when Jemmie's mother is able to offer help when Cass's younger sister suffers from heatstroke. (5–8)

Griffin, Adele. *Sons of Liberty.* Hyperion, 1998. ISBN 0-7868-0351-7
    Rock and Cliff Kindle are teenage boys who live with their abusive father and ineffective mother. They help a friend run away from an abusive stepfather. Next, they halfheartedly try to get their mother to come along as they plan their escape. Rock is a Civil War buff, and the book and chapter titles and other frequent references make that connection. (6–8)

Gundisch, Karin. *How I Became an American.* Cricket Books, 2001. ISBN 0-8126-4875-7
    This story follows the journey of a German family emigrating from Austria to America during the early 1900s. Mama asks Johnny (Johann on his birth certificate) to write everything down so that they will never forget their experiences. Johnny's father and eldest brother leave for Youngstown, Ohio, and then they send for the rest of the family. The journey is long and hard, and life in Youngstown is not easy. The children are able to adapt to the new lifestyle more easily than the parents. Batchelder Award winner. (4–7)

Hobbs, Valerie. *Carolina Crow Girl.* Farrar, Straus & Giroux, 2000. ISBN 0-374-3113-6
    Carolina and her mother, Melanie, and baby sister, Trinity, live in a old school bus. Melanie takes the family from place to place, and for a while they stay on oceanfront property that belongs to rich people. Carolina rescues a baby crow and cares for it until it is old enough to fly away. She meets wheelchair-bound Stefan, the son of the wealthy family who owns the land. Stefan's mother would like her to stay with them because she lost her daughter and would like Carolina to take her place. Carolina has some big decisions to make, and the crow helps her to make the right one when he chooses freedom. (5–8)

Mazer, Norma Fox. *Good Night Maman.* Harcourt Children's Books, 1999. ISBN 0-15-201468-3
    Karin is ten years old and hiding in an attic hidden from the occupying Germans with her brother and mother until they are forced to leave Paris and head south. When Maman becomes ill, Karin and her brother leave her behind and board a refugee ship bound for America in 1944. In the remainder of the novel, Karin and her brother adjust to the loneliness, surviving trauma and life in the refugee camp in Oswego, New York, until they leave to live with their aunt in California. (4–7)

Mead, Alice. *Junebug and the Reverend.* Farrar, Straus & Giroux, 1998. ISBN 0-374-33965-1
    Fourth-grader Junebug moves from the projects in New Haven, Connecticut, to an apartment building where his mother supervises some senior citizens. His new school has bullies; his mother has a new romance, and she makes him walk each day with the Reverend, an elderly patient, who is cranky and troublesome. Junebug is community-minded, kind to all, and very protective of his family. (4–6)

Metzger, Lois. *Missing Girls.* Penguin Putnam, 2001. ISBN 0-670-87777-8
    Carrie is sent to live with her grandmother for one year while her father works in another state. Her mother has died, and Carrie is in a dream state. She meets Mona, whose home life looks ideal to the casual observer. In time, Carrie sees the darkness in the modern lightness of Mona's home and the light in the darkness of her home with grandmother. She decides that she no longer wants to sleep away the rest of her life. (5–9)

Park, Linda Sue. *When My Name Was Keoko.* Clarion Books, 2002. ISBN 0-618-13335-6
    In 1940, the Japanese at the beginning of World War II, occupy Korea and force the Koreans to change their names to Japanese names and learn the Japanese language. A brother and sister try to go along with what is happening, but the sister keeps a forbidden journal and their uncle publishes a secret revolutionary newspaper. Her brother enlists in the Japanese army in the hope of protecting them. (5–9)

Rinaldi, Ann. *Keep Smiling Through.* Harcourt Children's Books, 1996. ISBN 0-15-200768-7
This historical novel describes the home front during World War II with all the patriotic efforts of the citizens to support the troops from scrap-metal drives to patriotic songs. Ten-year-old Kay is the youngest of her siblings in a household with a miserly father and a cruel stepmother. Kay keeps trying to do the right thing and keeps smiling through all the difficulties she has to face. (5–8)

Ryan, Pam Muñoz. *Esperanza Rising.* Scholastic, 2000. ISBN 0-439-12041-1
Esperanza thinks life will always be the same. She is brought up on the El Rancho de las Rosas in Mexico, which has vineyards and faithful servants. This changes when her father is shot and their family home is burned. They must flee to California. They are indebted to their former servants who help Esperanza and her mother find work on a farm in the San Joaquin Valley. Esperanza means "hope," and she remembers her *abuelita* saying to her, "Do not ever be afraid to start over." (6–9)

YA (grades 8–12)

Bell, Hilari. *A Matter of Profit.* HarperCollins, 2001. ISBN 0-06-029514-7
Forty planets and their inhabitants have joined together to form the T'Chin Confederation. Suddenly, without reason, they all surrender to the Vivitare forces. They learn that there is a plot to kill the emperor, so eighteen-year-old Ahvrene, is asked by his father to find out who is behind this plot. Ahvren hopes that if he solves this mystery then his sister will be free and not be forced to marry the emperor's evil son. (7–up)

 There can be no daily democracy without daily citizenship.
—Ralph Nader

Brenaman, Miriam. *Evvy's Civil War.* G. P. Putnam's Sons, 2002. ISBN 0-399-23713-5
Evvy is the eldest of five sisters, and when she turns fourteen, she is expected to act like a southern lady. However, when her father leaves to fight in the Civil War, the running of the plantation and small school is left up to her. (7–10)

Clement-Davies, David. *Fire Bringer.* Dutton Children's Books, 2000. ISBN 0-525-46492-1
The tale takes place in medieval Scotland when Rannoch, a buck, is born on the night his father is murdered. He has magical powers, and his mother sends him off with another herd for safety. Rannoch finally defeats the power-hungry buck who is trying to conquer all the deer and make them militia-minded. Rannoch frees the herd and becomes their leader. (7–12)

Deuker, Carl. *Runner.* Houghton Mifflin, 2005. ISBN 0-618-54298-1
Chance is given the opportunity to earn money for doing what he loves—running. He needs the money to pay the rent and buy food and other incidentals. Chance lives aboard a sailboat with his father who is an alcoholic. His father has lost his job once again, and Chance knows he must make money. He also knows that the packages he picks up on his runs probably contain drugs. Gradually, he realizes that he is smuggling more than drugs and that his life is getting away from him. (YA)

Hansen, Joyce. *The Heart Calls Home.* Walker, 1999. ISBN 0-8027-8636-7
This final book in a trilogy begins in South Carolina in 1866. Obi is a member of the black segment of the Union Army and is trying to find his three friends who are escaped slaves. He starts his own carpentry business while trying to entice Easter, one of his friends, to return to

marry him. Easter has gone away to Philadelphia to be educated as a teacher. Obi endures storms, disease, and bigotry as he tries to help war-orphaned children. (7–up)

Lynch, Chris. *Freewill*. HarperCollins, 2001. ISBN 0-06-028176-6
This story is about Will, a disturbed young man, who refers to himself as "you" throughout the novel. It is thought that his father accidentally drove off the road and into the water with Will's stepmother—but did he? Will finds himself in an occupational woodworking shop for emotionally disturbed teenagers where he spends his time making gnomes. When these gnomes begin to appear at the scene of teen suicides, Will starts to question himself. Michael L. Printz Honor Book. (8–up)

Pullman, Philip. *The Subtle Knife*. Random House, 1997. ISBN 0-679-80211-8
Second in the His Dark Materials trilogy, this story has Will Perry trying to find his father who is missing while exploring in the far north. Mysterious strangers pester his mother wanting news of him; Will accidentally kills one of the strangers and then escapes into another world. There he gets help from Lyra Silvertongue with his quest to find his father. Will soon acquires the subtle knife, a magical tool that will protect Will and Lyra on the quest to find his father. (7–12)

Turner, Megan Whalen. *The Thief*. HarperCollins, 1996. ISBN 0-688-14627-9
Gen, who is serving a life sentence for theft, is given the opportunity for freedom if he steals a legendary stone for King Magus. (7–up)

Nonfiction

Adler, David A. *A Picture Book of Harriet Tubman*. Holiday House, 1992. ISBN 0-8234-0926-0
Harriet was the sixth of eleven children. She was often beaten by the mistress of the plantation where she was born. In 1844, Harriet married a free man, John Tubman, and made her plans to runaway. She traveled the Underground Railroad and made her way to Pennsylvania. Harriet lived until she was almost ninety years old. She was courageous and helped many slaves attain freedom as a conductor on the Underground Railroad. (2–4)

 Truth-telling, I have found, is the key to responsible citizenship. The thousands of criminals I have seen in forty years of law enforcement have had one thing in common: every single one was a liar.
—J. Edgar Hoover

Bierman, Carol. *Journey to Ellis Island: How My Father Came to America*. Hyperion, 1998. ISBN 0-7868-0377-0
Yehuda was bound for America with his mother and sister. He lost a finger when he was hit by a stray bullet as his family escaped the war. As a result, he kept his arm in a sling. When they reached New York Harbor, the inspectors came aboard and told the captain that Yehuda must be returned to Russia. The captain intervened, and Yehuda, his mother, and sister went to Ellis Island where they were checked by several doctors and allowed to stay. The epilogue continued to follow the life of Yehuda, who was the author's father. Family photographs enhance the illustrations. (4–8)

Bunting, Eve. *Dreaming of America: An Ellis Island Story*. Troll, 2000. ISBN 0-8167-6520-0
Annie Moore, age fourteen, left Ireland aboard the S.S. *Nevada* with her two younger brothers to reunite with her parents who had left Ireland three years previously. They cross the ocean

and arrive in New York Harbor on Annie's birthday. Annie makes history by being the first immigrant to enter America through Ellis Island. She is given a ten-dollar gold piece to commemorate the event. "A statue of Annie and her brothers stands on the quay at Cobh, Ireland, where their journey began. Another stands on Ellis Island, where their journey ended." (2–4)

Cohn, Amy L., and Suzy Schmidt. *Abraham Lincoln.* Scholastic, 2002. ISBN 0-590-93566-6
This short biography of Abraham Lincoln is told in a conversational tone and the text is enhanced with quotes. Full-page ink and watercolor illustrations are placed on opposing pages. (2–4)

Drummond, Allan. *Liberty!* Farrar, Straus & Giroux, 2002. ISBN 0-374-34385-3
Liberty! describes the dedication of *Liberty Enlightening the World,* the Statue of Liberty which is a gift from the people of France. (K–3)

Hopkins, Lee Bennett. *Home to Me: Poems across America.* Orchard, 2002. ISBN 0-439-34096-9
Original poetry by Jane Yolen, Joseph Bruchac, and Lee Bennett Hopkins about various locations across America. Each poem speaks about homes in a traditional and patriotic way. (1–5)

Johnson, Linda Carlson. *Our National Symbols.* Millbrook Press, 1992. ISBN 1-56294-108-9
Symbols are those items unique to one's nation. This book includes information about the symbols of our nation and why they are important to us. They include the Liberty Bell, national emblem, bald eagle, great seal, Uncle Sam, Statue of Liberty, and today's symbols. (2–4)

Kroll, Steven. *By the Dawn's Early Light.* Scholastic, 1994. ISBN 0-590-45054-9
Francis Scott Key was a Washington lawyer during the War of 1812. This is the story of how he writes the *Star Spangled Banner* the day after the British are unsuccessful in their attack on Baltimore, Maryland. (ps–3)

Maestro, Betsy. *Coming to America.* Scholastic, 1996. ISBN 0-590-44151-5
The author traces the history of immigration to America from the first nomads who travel the land bridge from Asia, Native American Indians, European explorers, and immigrants, black slaves, and numerous nationalities that come in search of a better life. (K–4)

McKissack, Patricia C. *Sojourner Truth: Ain't I a Woman?* Scholastic, 1992. ISBN 0-590-44690-8
Belle Hardenburgh was born a slave in New York in 1797. Belle was bought and sold several times until she finally escaped with her youngest child when she was thirty years old. In 1843, she selected a new name, Sojourner Truth, and went about doing the "lord's work," speaking against slavery and in favor of women's rights. (5–8)

Partridge, Elizabeth. *This Land Was Made for You and Me.* Viking, 2002. ISBN 0-670-03535-1
A biography of the life and songs of Woody Guthrie whose songs reflected the political and social conditions he witnessed and experienced. (6–12)

Penner, Lucille Recht. *The Statue of Liberty.* Random House, 1995. ISBN 0-679-86928-X
This is a Step into Reading book that briefly describes the history of the Statue of Liberty, a gift from the people of France. It was dedicated on October 28, 1886, and welcomed people of all nationalities to America. (K–1)

Ryan, Pam Muñoz. *The Flag We Love.* Charlesbridge, 1996. ISBN 0-88106-845-4
This picture book discusses the significance of our flag, how and where it is flown, and our national pride in our flag. (1–6)

Spencer, Eve. *A Flag for Our Country.* Raintree Steck-Vaughn, 1993. ISBN 0-8114-7211-6
This the story of Betsy Ross and what happened in 1776 when George Washington asked her to make a new flag to help the patriots win the War of Independence. (K–5)

St. Pierre, Stephanie. *Our National Anthem.* Millbrook Press, 1992. ISBN 1-56294-106-2

Our national anthem, *The Star Spangled Banner*, is a song to show our feelings and how proud we are of the United States. It was approved by the National Anthem Act of Congress in 1931. This book discusses the history and significance of our National Anthem and other patriotic songs. (3–5)

West, Delno C., and Jean M. West. *Uncle Sam and Old Glory.* Atheneum Children's Books for Young Readers, 2000. ISBN 0-689-82043-7

Symbols are an expression of who we are and what we stand for as Americans. This book explores "where our symbols come from, what they mean, and how they have come to identify us as Americans." (1–3)

Chapter *12*

Forgiveness

Related Virtues

Pardon, absolution, leniency, mercy, grace, harmony

Definition

Compassionate feelings that support a willingness to forgive, the act of excusing a mistake or offense

Forgiveness in Action

- ✧ Be forgiving of others.
- ✧ Be slow to take offense.
- ✧ Show mercy on others in sports and competitions.
- ✧ Be kind to those who are not as fortunate as you.
- ✧ Try to keep harmony with siblings.
- ✧ Lose gracefully.
- ✧ When you say "I'm sorry," make sure you mean it.

People Who Have Demonstrated This Virtue

- ✧ Mahatma Gandhi
- ✧ Jesus
- ✧ Anwar Sadat
- ✧ Elie Wiesel
- ✧ Madeline Albright

- ◇ Desmond Tutu
- ◇ Yitzhak Rabin

Discussion Questions

- ◇ Can it be harmful to you to be angry and full of hate?
- ◇ Are you angry with anyone right now?
- ◇ Why is it important to talk about your feelings?
- ◇ Is it easy to forgive?
- ◇ If you have done something hurtful to someone, what should you do?
- ◇ Do you sometimes say you are sorry but not mean it?
- ◇ Why is it difficult to admit to being wrong?
- ◇ Is it important to live in harmony with others?
- ◇ What about being in harmony with nature? Is that a good thing?

Related Topics to Explore

- ◇ Presidential pardons
- ◇ Amnesty
- ◇ Court system—leniency
- ◇ The Guardian Angels
- ◇ Death penalty
- ◇ Treatment of prisoners

Annotated Titles

Picture Books

Buehner, Mark. *I Did It, I'm Sorry.* Dial Books for Young Readers, 1998. ISBN 0-8037-2010-6
Readers are presented with an ethical situation and are asked to give the correct behavior or response from the three multiple choices. The correct letter is found in the accompanying pictures along with hidden animals. (K–3)

Climo, Shirley. *Atalanta's Race.* Clarion Books, 1995. ISBN 0-395-67322-4
When Atalanta is born, her father, King Iasus, is disappointed that she is a girl, so he casts her away on a mountainside. A she-bear hears her whimpering and places Atalanta with her cubs for the winter. A hunter stumbles upon the cave and baby. He raises Atalanta and teaches her how to hunt and take care of herself. After winning many awards for her athletic ability, she is summoned to King Iasus, and she learns of her biological father and her earlier fate. Princess Atalanta decides to stay and the king urges her to choose a husband and marry. She arranges a contest and decides that "he who loses will lose his head." Melanion, a young Greek warrior, is regarded as a hero and an athlete. Atalanta pleads with Melanion to withdraw from the race. With the help of Aphrodite, Melanion wins and marries Atalanta. However, they never offer appropriate thanks to Aphrodite and are turned into a lion and lioness. Atalanta's famous race is about the length of a present-day 1500-meter run. (3–7)

De Groat, Diane. *Roses Are Pink, Your Feet Really Stink.* HarperCollins, 1997. ISBN 0-688-15-2201

Gilbert is writing something nice on all his Valentines to his classmates—except those for Margaret and Lewis. Margaret and Lewis are both mean to Gilbert, so he writes a nasty saying on each Valentine and signs it by each other's name. When it is time for the class to open their Valentines, all are happy except for Lewis and Margaret. They get into a fight, and the class is punished. When Margaret looks at her Valentine again, she realizes that she has two from Lewis, one nice and one mean. It becomes obvious that Gilbert is the one who wrote the mean Valentine. When they ask Gilbert why, he tells them about the time they were mean to him. Lewis and Margaret apologize to Gilbert, and in art class Gilbert makes new Valentines, nice ones this time. (K–2)

Durant, Alan. *Big Bad Bunny.* Dutton Children's Books, 2000. ISBN 0-525-46667-3

No one is safe from Big Bad Bunny who wants their money, until he meets Wise Old Bunny who covers Big Bad Bunny with bags of money. Big Bad Bunny promises to give back what he takes and surprises his friends with a pie from a Very Good Bunny. (ps–1)

A forgiveness ought to be like a canceled note, torn in two and burned up, so that it never can be shown against the man.
—Henry Ward Beecher

Gantos, Jack. *Rotten Ralph's Rotten Romance.* Houghton Mifflin, 1997. ISBN 0-395-73978-0

It is Valentine's Day and Ralph is his rotten self, especially at Petunia's party. When it is all over, Sarah makes Ralph take a bath and then she forgives him—after all, Ralph is her favorite Valentine. (ps–3)

Kassirer, Sue. *Joseph and His Coat of Many Colors.* Aladdin Paperbacks, 1997. ISBN 0-689-81226-4

This biblical Joseph is betrayed by his brothers and sold into Egyptian slavery. Later in a time of famine, Joseph forgives his brothers, provides food, and becomes a great ruler. (00–3)

Munson, Derek. *Enemy Pie.* Chronicle Books, 2000. ISBN 0-8118-2778-X

It is going to be a great summer until Jeremy moves into the neighborhood and becomes his neighbor's number-one enemy. Dad suggests to his son that they make enemy pie, but for it to work he has to spend the day playing with the enemy and acting like he is having good time. The little boy soon learns that he has lost his best enemy and that enemy pie is delicious. (K–3)

Primary (grades 1–3)

Bunting, Eve. *So Far from the Sea.* Clarion Books, 1998. ISBN 0-395-72095-8

Young Laura and her family are moving from California to Boston, but before they do, they visit the Manzanar War Relocation Center. Laura's father was a young boy when he and his parents were relocated to the center after the Japanese bombed Pearl Harbor. Years later, the family visits the monument with the words "Memorial to the Dead" and leaves flowers on her grandfather's grave. Laura leaves a special symbol at the grave and realizes that some things cannot be changed but that one must move on. (2–5)

Byars, Betsy. *My Brother, Ant.* Viking Children's Books, 1996. ISBN 0-670-86664-4
An easy-to-read chapter book divided into four stories about a big brother's caring and patience with his little brother, Ant. He forgives Ant for drawing on his homework, helps Ant rid a monster from under the bed, attempts to read Ant a story, and helps Ant write a letter to Santa in July. (00–3)

Forgiveness is a gift of high value. Yet its cost is nothing.
—Betty Smith

Goble, Paul. *Star Boy.* Aladdin Paperbacks, 1991. ISBN 0-689-71499-8
A Blackfoot Indian legend about Star Boy, son of Morning Star and grandson of the sun and moon asks his grandfather's permission to marry the chief's daughter. The sun grants permission and tells Star Boy to tell the people to build a lodge each summer, and then the sun will give back health to the sick people. Long after Star Boy dies, the people continue to build a special lodge in honor of the sun. "The people dance and give thanks, and pray that the Creator will take away their scars and make their heats new again just as Star Boy was made new a long time ago." (ps–3)

Howe, James. *Pinky and Rex and the School Play.* Atheneum Children's Books, 1998. ISBN 0-689-31872-3
Pinky and Rex are best friends, but maybe not for long. Pinky hopes to be an actor when he grows up and tries out for the school play. Rex, on the other hand, has no real interest and just tries out to support her friend. To their surprise, Rex is picked to be the lead in the play, and Pinky gets the part of a monkey. Will they remain friends? (K–3)

Perrault, Charles. *Cinderella and Other Tales from Perrault.* Henry Holt, 1989. ISBN 0-8050-1004-1
Cinderella is as kind as she is beautiful and lives happily ever after. She forgives her stepsisters and arranges marriages for them with great lords. (2–4)

Intermediate (grades 3–5)

Bradley, Kimberly Brubaker. *Halfway to the Sky.* Delacorte Press, 2002. ISBN 0-385-72960-X
Dani set out to be a thru-hiker, one who walks the entire Appalachian Trail from Springer Mountain, Georgia, to Mount Kathadin, Maine. Many years ago, her parents walked the Appalachian Trail, fell in love, married, and had a son, Springer, and a daughter, Kathadin—Dani. When her brother dies, and her father leaves, the only thing Dani can do is run away to the Appalachian Trail. Her mother finds her and agrees to walk the trail for two months because that is all the time she can take from work. Together they walk 695 miles and work out their anger and sorrow over Springer's death. Dani knows that in time she will complete all 2,167 miles. (3–7)

Fleischman, Sid. *Bo and Mzzz Mad.* Harper Trophy, 2001. ISBN 0-06-029397-7
Bo arrives at his distant relative's home in the Mojave Desert after his poet father dies in a motorcycle accident. These are the only relatives he has, and Bo knows about the feud that has kept the families apart. After a cool reception, Bo decides that he will leave until two unlikely hoodlums show up with designs to find the lost Pegleg Smith Mine. Bo saves his relatives by sending the hoodlums on a wild goose chase. In the process, Bo finds an unlikely family, information that solves the family rift, and a picture of his great-great-grandfather, which is a map of the mine. (3–up)

Henkes, Kevin. *Sun & Spoon.* Greenwillow Books, 1997. ISBN 0-688-15232-5

 Ten-year-old Spoon misses his deceased grandmother and is afraid that he will forget her so he takes her deck of cards as a memento so that his memories will not fade. His grandfather misses the cards as he is comforted by using them. Spoon confesses that he is the one who took the cards and finds something better to remember her by. (3–5)

 Forgiveness is the act of admitting we are like other people.
        —Christina Baldwin

Kurtz, Ann. *I'm Sorry, Almira Ann.* Henry Holt, 1999. ISBN 0-8050-6094-4

 Eight-year-old Sarah and Almira Ann share the same birthday with America, the fourth of July. They grow up together, and now both families are packing to head west on the Oregon Trail. Sarah has a wild streak that often gets her into trouble. Almira Ann and Sarah's brother are playing in the back of the wagon, and Sarah is feeling envious and left out of their game. She pulls a quilt over her head and in a quiet moment flings the quilt off and lets out a blood curdling scream. Almira Ann falls backward out of the moving wagon and one of the wheels rolls over her leg. Without a doctor, how is Almira Ann going to proceed on the wagon trip to Oregon? Sarah doesn't know how she will be able to face Almira Ann again. How can she show her how truly sorry she is, and will Almira Ann forgive her? (2-4)

Lasky, Kathryn. *Dreams in the Golden Country: The Diary of Zipporah Feldman, A Jewish Immigrant Girl.* Scholastic, 1998. ISBN 0-590-02973-8

 Zipporah is twelve years old and an immigrant from Russia. The diary entries document the first eighteen months of her life in the United States, beginning with Ellis Island and then life in the Lower East Side of New York City in the early 1900s. (4–9)

Polacco, Patricia. *Pink and Say.* Scholastic, 1998. ISBN 0-439-04467-7

 Sheldon Curtis or Say is a wounded Union soldier on a Georgia battlefield when Pinkus Aylee finds him and brings him home to be nursed by Moe Moe Bay. Pink, a black Union soldier, is anxious to get back to his outfit. Say is afraid and asks God's forgiveness because he doesn't ever want to go back. Confederate marauders kill Moe Moe Bay, and Pink and Say are caught and sent to Andersonville. Only Say survives. The book is dedicated to Pinkus Aylee. Say is the great-grandfather of Patricia Polacco. (K–5)

Middle School (grades 5–8)

Brooke, Peggy. *Jake's Orphan.* Dorling Kindersley, 2000. ISBN 0-7894-2628-5

 Tree is twelve years old, and Acorn is his ten-year-old brother. They are orphans in Minnesota in 1926. Tree has a chance to be adopted and become part of a family when he is sent to the Gunderson Farm in North Dakota to work for a year. Mr. Gunderson is strict, and Tree has to work very hard. When Acorn runs away and shows up at the farm, Mr. Gunderson decides that the boys will be sent back to the orphanage since the year is up. Acorn's disruptive behavior and scheming ways make matters worse. Mr. Gunderson's bachelor brother defends the boys and becomes their legal guardian. (5–9)

Calvert, Patricia. *Glennis, Before & After.* Atheneum Children's Books for Young Readers, 1996. ISBN 0-689-80641-8

 Glennis, twelve years old, is faced with a very difficult situation. Her father is jailed for a white-collar crime, and her mother has a nervous breakdown. So Glennis, her brother, and three sisters go in different directions to live with extended family members. Glennis selects Aunt

Wanda, the first black sheep of the family, as her foster parent, because she lives near the detention center where her father is incarcerated. She visits him regularly but is distraught yet again when he tells her he's guilty. She stops visiting him and turns her attention toward Aunt Wanda and her cousin, Skipper, in a futile attempt to get her family back on track again. (5–8)

Friesen, Gayle. *Janey's Girl.* Kids Can Press, 1998. ISBN 1-5507-4461-5
Claire and her mother travel across country to visit Claire's grandmother in British Columbia. Once there, Claire tries to find out about her family, especially her dad whom she has never known. She finds out that a divorced man, living in the town with his son, is her father. Her mother is still very angry about her association with Claire's father. The brief relationship ended when, as a teenager, her mother became pregnant. It is a coming-of-age story for both Claire and her mother. (6–9)

Forgiveness is the fragrance the violet sheds on the heel that has crushed it.
—Mark Twain

Griffin, Adele. *The Other Shepards.* Hyperion, 1998. ISBN 0-7868-1333-4
Before Geneva and Holland were born, a drunk driver kills their sister and two brothers when they were teenagers. Its effects are manifested in the compulsive behaviors of Geneva, a sixth grader, and Holland, an eighth grader. At first glance, it appears that Geneva is the one most disturbed by events over which she had no control. Holland is the older sister who looks out for her. As the story progresses, it is Geneva who is the key to both of the girls' recovery from the strain and burden of grief that fills their lives. Through the guidance of Annie who arrives to paint a mural in their home, the girls gradually and courageously leave their grief behind and begin to experience life again. Is Annie an imaginary friend or the ghost of their dead sister Elizabeth Ann? (4–7)

Hesse, Karen. *Out of the Dust.* Scholastic, 1997. ISBN 0-590-36080-9
This is one year in the life of fourteen-year-old Billy Jo. She lives on a farm during the Great Depression in the Oklahoma dust bowl. After fourteen years, her Ma is pregnant. Ma copes with the dust and accepts a position in life that is less than what she had hoped. On a day in July, Daddy puts a pail of kerosene next to the stove. Ma, thinking it is water, begins to pour it to make coffee, but instead, "Ma made a rope of fire." Ma runs outside screaming for Daddy. Billy Jo grabs the kerosene pail and throws it out the door. Unbeknownst to Billy Jo, Ma is returning to the kitchen, and the burning kerosene goes all over her. Ma is burned all down the front of her and Billy Jo, who has had a promising career as a pianist, burns her hands. Ma and the baby brother both die a month later in childbirth. There is no one to raise and comfort Billy Jo. Her father barely talks because he is so involved in his own grief and maintaining the farm during the drought. Billy Jo is so desperate to leave that she catches a freight train west. She arrives in Arizona and realizes that getting away isn't any better. She decides to return home. At last, she forgives Daddy for leaving the kerosene pail and forgives herself for all that happened later. Newbery Award winner. (5–8)

Paterson, Katherine. *Parzival: The Quest of the Grail Knight.* Lodestar Books, 1998. ISBN 0-525-67579-5
This is an abridged rendition of a thirteenth-century pre-Galahad Arthurian legend. Parzival, who has royal blood but is raised as a peasant, sets off to seek adventure without knowing who he really is. At Arthur's court, he wins Red Knight's armor in a dual. He goes from adventure to adventure, and during a quest to find the keeper of the Holy Grail and break a curse, he commits

a near-tragic error. He struggles for a long time to atone for his mistake and eventually becomes a respected hero. (5–up)

Taylor, Theodore. *A Sailor Returns.* Blue Sky Press, 2001. ISBN 0-4392-4879-5
   Eleven-year-old Evan and his mother are both surprised when Evan receives a letter from his grandfather who has been missing for more than thirty years. He asks to visit his long lost daughter and grandson. It is summer vacation, and Evan can't wait for his grandfather's visit. Grandfather tells Evan and his friend stories and goes fishing with them. When there is a murder investigation, it is revealed that Evan's grandfather committed a murder long ago in self-defense. He is afraid that his family will not forgive him, but they do. (4–8)

Vos, Ida. *Anna Is Still Here.* Houghton Mifflin, 1993. ISBN 0-395-65368-1
   When the Germans occupy Holland, Anna is alone hiding in an attic. For three years, she speaks to no one. Now that they are free, Anna has nightmares, occasionally speaks softly, and is convinced that one German was left behind in the white house at the end of the street. Anna meets Mrs. Neumann who lives in the white house. Mrs. Neumann flees Germany in 1937 and is in hiding with her husband and daughter in Holland when she is forced to go the dentist. While there, her husband and daughter are rounded up by the Nazis. Mrs. Neumann has problems adjusting and is still waiting for her husband and daughter to come home. Anna and Mrs. Neumann begin to talk to each other about their experiences in the war. Together they help each other mend. (3–7)

YA (grades 8–12)

Bloor, Edward. *Tangerine.* Scholastic, 1997. ISBN 0-439-28603-4
   This Florida author tells the story of Paul Fisher who wears thick glasses because of an earlier eye injury and his older brother Erik, who is a high school football star. Gradually the story unfolds about the relationship between the two boys and Paul's mysterious eye injury. Despite his injury, Paul sees everything, even things his parents can't or won't see. (7–12)

Cooney, Caroline B. *The Voice on the Radio.* Delacorte Press, 1996. ISBN 0-385-32213-5
   Janie Johnson's boyfriend Reeve, a college freshman, tries to make a name for himself at the campus radio station. He decides to treat listeners to brief vignettes of Janie's strange history. Janie is trying to adjust to her birth family, the Springs. She goes with them on a trip to visit colleges and hears Reeve's program while she is in Boston to see him. She discusses all this with Mrs. Spring, her biological mother. Will she forgive Reeve? (6–10)

Frank, E. R. *America.* Atheneum Children's Books for Young Readers, 2002. ISBN 0-689-84729-7
   America's brutal life is told in alternating chapters of then and now. The "then" refers to his birth to a drug-addicted mother and how he was given to the welfare system at a young age. He was in various foster homes and then eventually lost in the system for eleven years. The "now" refers to America's attempt at suicide and his rehabilitation and therapy in a residential psychiatric program. With the help of a dedicated and caring social worker, America might just be able to pick up the pieces, forgive, and forget. (8–up)

Mazer, Norma Fox. *When She Was Good.* Arthur A. Levine Books, 1997. ISBN 0-590-13506-6
   Em Thurkill is the daughter of an alcoholic, abusive father and a silent, depressed mother. Her older sister becomes mentally ill and abuses Em for three long years before the sister dies. Em realizes in the end that she can forgive and get on with her life. (8–up)

Mikaelson, Ben. *Touching Spirit Bear.* HarperCollins, 2001. ISBN 0-380-97744-3
   Cole Matthews is a bully with so much anger inside that he viciously beats a ninth-grade classmate—a beating so brutal it results in brain damage. Cole faces a prison sentence but is offered an alternative: Circle Justice. He is happy to take this opportunity instead of prison because

he still blames everyone but himself for the things that happen and feels this will be much easier than serving time in prison. Circle Justice is based on Native American tradition, and Cole is banished, alone, to a remote Alaskan island for a year. Cole has an encounter with a Spirit Bear and is badly mauled and left for dead. After finally being rescued, he spends six months recovering from his injuries, and during that time he realizes he must control his anger and change his ways. (5–up)

Rinaldi, Ann. *Broken Days: The Quilt Trilogy #2.* Scholastic, 1999. ISBN 0-590-46053-6
   The setting is Massachusetts in the days before the War of 1812. Walking Breeze, who is half Shawnee, is the daughter of Thankful Chelmsford. When her mother dies, Walking Breeze goes to live with family in Salem and finds her new life totally different from her life in the Shawnee village. Cousin Ebie Chelmsford, an insecure teen, makes an accusation that Walking Breeze is not really Thankful's daughter because she is afraid that Walking Breeze will become her grandmother's favorite. (6–up)

Wild, Margaret. *Jinx.* Simon & Schuster, 2004. ISBN 0-68-987-1171
   Poems of varying length relate the story of Jen, who thinks she is a jinx. First she deals with the tragic unrelated deaths of two consecutive boyfriends and her parents divorce after her sister is born "imperfect." She also deals with her friend Ruth who is brutally honest, Connie, a lesbian, and Serena, who wants to be noticed. (9–up, for mature readers)

Nonfiction

Demi. *Gandhi.* Margaret K. McElderry Books, 2001. ISBN 0-689-84149-3
   Gandhi was a shy man who married according to custom when he was thirteen years old. He went to London and studied law. He experienced racism when in 1893 he went to work in South Africa. He created the theory of *satyagraha,* or the force of selfless love, which advocates love and peace to overcome violence. Gandhi returned to India in 1915 and worked to rid India of its caste system and of British oppression. (2–5)

 The weak can never forgive. Forgiveness is the attribute of the strong.
   —Mahatma Gandhi

Nir, Yehuda. *The Lost Childhood: A World War II Memoir.* Scholastic, 2002. ISBN 0-439-16389-7
   Nir is nine years when Poland was invaded by Nazi Germany. Two years later, he saw his father wounded with other Jewish men and then shot. Nir, his mother, and his sister went on the run, eluded capture, and managed to obtain papers so that they could pass as Catholics. (7–12)

Schuman, Michael A. *Elie Wiesel: Voice from the Holocaust.* Enslow, 1994. ISBN 0- 89490-428-0
   Elie Wiesel was sent with his family to the Auschwitz concentration camp and later to Buchenwald until he was liberated at age sixteen. As an adult, he became a writer, teacher, philosopher, and winner of the Nobel Peace Prize in 1986. He "swore never to be silent whenever and wherever human beings endure suffering and humiliation." (5–8)

Warren, Andrea. *Surviving Hitler: A Boy in the Nazi Death Camps.* HarperCollins, 2001. ISBN 0-06-029218-0
   This biography of Jack Mandelbaum is reconstructed from his memories and interviews with the author. When he is fifteen years old, Jack was separated from the rest of his family and sent to the Blechhammer concentration camp until he was freed three years later. Jack says that he would not have tried so hard to stay alive if he had known the fate of the rest of his family. (5–up)

Author Index

Title Index

About the Authors

LIZ KNOWLES, Ed.D., is Director of Staff Development at Pine Crest School, Boca Raton, Florida. Liz and Martha have published several books with Libraries Unlimited including *Reading Rules!*, which received an award from IRA and the recent *Boys and Literacy*.

MARTHA SMITH is Library Media Specialist, Pine Crest School, Boca Raton, Florida.